ECONOMIC
PARABLES
& POLICIES

ECONOMIC PARABLES & POLICIES

Saving for America's Economic Future

Laurence S. Seidman

M.E. Sharpe

Armonk, New York
London, England

Library of Congress Cataloging-in-Publication Data

Seidman, Laurence S.
Economic parables and policies : saving for America's economic
future / Laurence S. Seidman. — 2nd ed.
p.   cm.
Rev. ed. of: Saving for America's economic future. 1990.
Includes index.
ISBN 0–7656–0240–7 (hardcover : alk. paper). —
ISBN 0–7656–0241–5 (pbk. : alk. paper)
1. United States—Economic policy—1981–1993.
I. Seidman, Laurence S. Saving for America's economic future.
II. Title.
HC106.8.S44 1998
338.973′009′048—dc21   97–36960
CIP

Printed in the United States of America

The paper used in this publication meets the minimum requirements of
American National Standard for Information Sciences—
Permanence of Paper for Printed Library Materials,
ANSI Z 39.48-1984.

BM (c)   10   9   8   7   6   5   4   3   2   1
BM (p)   10   9   8   7   6   5   4   3   2   1

For my parents,
Eleanor and Irving Seidman

CONTENTS

PREFACE

This is a serious book about a serious subject. But that doesn't mean that every page must contain the serious terms of formal economics. This book tries to challenge the conventional wisdom about substance: It delineates economic policies we can adopt to meet our economic challenges. But it also tries to challenge the conventional wisdom about style: It sets forth a serious analysis in a lighter vein.

Can good economics be entertaining—at least some of the time? Is it possible to learn economics while smiling—at least occasionally? Can economic policies be made interesting—at least most of the time? I believe the answer to these questions is yes. That's why I've written this book from the point of view that economics is potentially enjoyable as well as serious and important.

As we approach the year 2000, there is deep concern about our nation's economic future. How can we meet our economic challenges? How can we save America's economic future? And how can we do it while improving the fairness of our society?

I try to give serious answers to these questions. But please note the cast of characters that try to make my answers more enjoyable and memorable: Adam and Eve (chapter 1), Senator

Myopia and Old Karl (chapter 2), emaciated S and the lazy heir (chapter 3), the passionate objector (chapter 4), Ricardo (chapter 7), the Tryers (chapter 8), Senator Economus (chapter 10), and XT (chapter 11). Every chapter strives for a light, conversational exposition of a serious subject.

As a professor of economics, I spend most of my time writing technical articles for economics journals and teaching college students from textbooks (I've written one myself). I believe strongly that we academics, immersed in technical work, should occasionally take time out to communicate to a wider audience. After all, if we don't, there are others whose skill at writing far surpasses their knowledge of economics and who will be glad to entertain and mislead that wider audience. So I've tried to make this serious subject accessible and enjoyable. I hope you find it stimulating.

I am deeply indebted to the articles and books of economists too numerous to name. Don't let the absence of footnotes and endnotes mislead you. They are omitted because they would take up too much space. So here's a heartfelt thanks to my fellow economists. I owe a special debt to my colleague and research partner, Ken Lewis.

I want to thank Kim Whitesel for secretarial assistance in preparing the computer disks.

The book is dedicated to my parents, Eleanor and Irving Seidman, who have given me the foundation that shapes this book. I have some hope that my brothers, Leon and Robbie, will read it. I owe thanks to my father-in-law, Richard Kane, for helpful discussions, and have some hope that my mother-in-law, Mary Kane, will read it. Finally, I am most grateful to my daughter, Suzanna, my son, Jesse, and my wife, Ann.

ECONOMIC
PARABLES
&
POLICIES

1 AN ECONOMIST'S GENESIS

In the beginning, Adam and Eve had no tools. To compensate, God saw to it that the weather and soil never failed them. Initially, Adam and Eve devoted all their working time to growing food. With their bare hands, they plowed, planted, and harvested. Each year, they consumed all the food they produced, and each year, production and consumption remained the same. For all we know, Adam and Eve were happy.

Adam's Dream

But one night, Adam had a dream. With an imagination that leaped centuries, Adam dreamed of a tractor. In the dream, Adam saw their ability to plow, plant, and harvest multiply.

"If only we had a tractor." The thought haunted Adam and Eve for weeks as they continued to farm with their bare hands. Naturally, they prayed daily to God to give them a tractor. But to no avail.

One day, Adam and Eve were walking in the garden.

"So you want a tractor?" spoke a voice. And they knew the voice was God's.

"Yes," they replied, trembling. And God answered, "Do you

expect a tractor to fall from the sky like manna from Heaven?"

And Adam and Eve whispered, "That's exactly what we were hoping."

Then God laughed, and in a kind voice said, "No, my children, it is time for you to eat from the tree of economic knowledge. I will not give you a tractor. You must make your own tractor, by the sweat of your brow."

"That's just what we were afraid of," said Adam and Eve. Then God burned detailed instructions—"How to Make a Tractor"—onto a tablet of stone that lay at the foot of the tree of economic knowledge. As they sat under the tree, eating its fruit and reading the instructions, Adam and Eve suddenly realized a fundamental truth of the human condition. They realized that, while making a tractor, they must devote less time to plowing, planting, and harvesting food. In the short run, they must reduce their consumption of food.

"We face a trade-off," said Eve suddenly. "We must sacrifice consumption in the present, while we build the tractor, in order to enjoy more consumption in the future."

"Isn't there any way around this?" asked Adam gloomily.

"I'm afraid not," said Eve, who may have been the second person, but was clearly the first economist. "No sacrifice, no rise in the standard of living. It's that simple, honey."

The Ritual

Having eaten from the tree of economic knowledge, Adam and Eve decided to do their accounting properly. Although they knew it was unnecessary in their simple economy, they decided it would be fun to use money to keep track and, more important, to help their descendants understand the fundamentals. Conveniently, identical rectangular-shaped green leaves hung from the branches of the tree of economic knowledge. By fiat, Adam and Eve declared each leaf to be one dollar ($1). Here's how they did their accounting.

They began with the pre-tractor economy. Each year they produced a hundred units of food. They arbitrarily declared the price per unit of food to be $1, so that total output (which they also called *gross domestic product,* or *GDP*) was $100.

To illustrate a basic truth of national income accounting, Adam and Eve engaged in a ritual. Playing the role of consumers, they paid $100 for the food, which they called *output,* placing the hundred leaves on a flat boulder beneath the tree of economic knowledge. Immediately, they circled to the opposite side of the boulder to play the role of producers, and promptly picked up the hundred leaves, thereby receiving $100 of *income* from the sale of the food.

"What a coincidence," said Adam. "We bought $100 of output, and also received exactly $100 of income."

With patience and sensitivity, Eve made her husband see that it had to be so. "Output equals income," whispered Eve softly. "It's our first accounting identity."

They also noted that in the pre-tractor economy, total consumption was equal to total output—$100.

Then Eve said, "Let's *assume* we built a tractor this year."

"But we didn't," Adam objected.

"I'm an economist," Eve retorted. "I can assume anything I want. Now let's redo our accounting. Assume we devoted 40 percent of our work time to the construction of one tractor. Then our time spent on food production fell 40 percent, so food output fell from a hundred to sixty units."

As good accountants, they reasoned as follows. Since the total labor time devoted to all production (food plus tractor) was the same, total output should still be valued at $100. Since output of the consumer good fell from $100 to $60, the price of the tractor should be set at $40, so that total output would remain $100.

"Let's call food the 'consumer' good," expounded Eve, "because it is used up—consumed—in the year it is produced. Let's call the tractor the *investment* good, because it raises productive power in future years.

"I have another accounting identity," she then exclaimed. "Output ($100) equals consumption ($60) plus investment ($40)."

Then they performed their ritual at the boulder under the tree. Two goods were now available for sale: the consumer good (food), and the investment good (the tractor). Playing the role of consumers, Adam and Eve paid $60 for the food. Playing the role of investors, they paid $40 for the tractor. Immediately, they circled to the opposite side of the boulder and, as producers, promptly received $100 of income.

"Notice," said Eve, "that we consumed $40 less than our income; our income was $100, and our consumption was only $60. I propose that we *define* income minus consumption to be *saving*. Our saving, therefore, was $40."

"What a coincidence," said Adam. "Our investment was also $40."

Once again, with gentle patience, Eve tried to explain to her husband that it had to be so, that saving had to equal investment. But this time she found it harder to make him grasp the point.

Suddenly she exclaimed, "A bank! I'll show him with a bank."

Eve promptly declared a nearby boulder to be a bank. She said to Adam, "Let's do the ritual again."

But this time when, as producers, they received the $100 of income, Eve said to her husband, "Let's save $40 of our income. Let's put $40 in that bank over there."

She led Adam by the hand to the bank and deposited the $40 on top of the bank boulder. "We've just saved $40 of our income. We'll consume the remaining $60.

"Now," she said, "let's play the role of investors who want to buy the tractor. We'll borrow $40 from the bank." At the bank boulder, she took the $40 that had been saved and, leading Adam back to the original boulder, used the $40 to buy the tractor.

"Investment equals saving," she whispered softly. "It's our third accounting identity."

Then Eve sat under the tree of economic knowledge, lost in thought. Suddenly, she jumped to her feet.

"Do you realize what this means, dear husband? Investment, unlike consumption, raises our future productive power. But to invest, we must save. And saving means consuming less than our income."

"And there isn't any way around it?" asked Adam once again.

"None whatsoever," replied Eve. "You don't get something for nothing," she added, her cheerful tone confirming that she was, indeed, the first economist.

Adam grumbled, "You certainly do practice a dismal science."

Optimal Saving in a Lonely Eden

Adam paced anxiously under the tree of economic knowledge.

"What's the matter, dear?" asked Eve.

Adam's eyes darted in all directions.

"I don't think I want to build the tractor," he confessed guilt-ily. "Of course, I want the tractor. But I don't want to save for the tractor. I can't bear to cut my consumption," he blurted out, tears streaming down his face.

"There, there, dear," Eve comforted him. "I know how much trips to our little food mall mean to you. You've become quite attached to it."

"I'm addicted to it," Adam cried out in despair. "I don't think I can survive a cut in my consumption, even for one year. Eve, I need a compassionate therapist, and curse my lot, the only other living being is an economist."

Without taking offense, Eve replied, "Now, dear, I know what you've heard about economists—that they are devoid of emotion, that they depict man as a calculating robot, that all they care about are dollars and cents. But you forget that all this came later, after Adam Smith glorified the virtues of specialization. For God's sake, this is Eden, we're the only two people on earth—at least, as far as we know—so I can't afford to be only an economist. I also have a degree in psychology. Let me help. Here, lie down on this couch, and try to relax."

Eve's tender, soothing voice convinced Adam that she was, indeed, more than just an economist. Maybe she could help him with his overwhelming guilt. Adam lay down, without even asking where the couch came from.

"Eve," Adam confessed, "I know that economics teaches that saving is always better than consuming. I know my lust for consumption is wrong. But I can't repress it."

"Adam, this may come as a pleasant shock to you, but that is not what modern economics teaches. Saving is not always better than consuming."

Adam was indeed shocked. "I don't understand," he gasped with relief.

"Believe it or not," Eve continued, "economics cannot tell you whether to save or not. Economics simply shows you the consequence. It's then up to you to decide."

"What do you mean by 'consequence'?" Adam asked.

"Well," answered Eve, "here's how an economist would help you make your decision. First, she would ask: Once the tractor is built, how much will it raise food output in each future year?"

"In my dream, " Adam replied, "the tractor raised food output $20 per year, forever."

"How convenient that God has not yet cursed mankind with depreciation," Eve laughed. "Since the tractor lasts forever—it never depreciates, or wears out—we can easily compute the *rate of return* on our saving. The tractor will cost us $40 of consumption, but it will then yield a return of $20 per year, so the rate of return is $20 divided by $40, or 50 percent."

Agitated, Adam asked, "Doesn't economics teach that you should save if the rate of return is 50 percent?"

"No," Eve replied in a soothing voice. "Economics simply asks you to compare, in your mind, two situations. Under the first, without the tractor, you consume $100 of food in every year. Under the second, with the tractor, you consume $60 in the first year, and then $120 in all future years. Economics then says that there is no right or wrong choice. Whatever you decide is OK with economics. Just as economics does not presume to tell you whether to eat fewer apples and more oranges, so economics does not presume to tell you whether to consume less in the present and more in the future."

"You mean, economics accepts *consumer sovereignty* and applies the principle to present vs. future consumption, as well as to apples vs. oranges?" Adam asked with a feeling of relief.

"Yes," Eve laughed, gently wiping the perspiration off her husband's forehead with a fig leaf. "You can check any standard economics text."

"So I can decide whatever I want, as long as I recognize the trade-off, and economics will not condemn me?" asked Adam joyfully.

"Yes, my love," Eve replied.

"Oh Eve, please, can we forget the tractor? I just can't bear to cut consumption below $100, even if the return on my saving is 50 percent."

"Move over," whispered Eve, and within moments the two had forgotten the tractor.

Far East of Eden

And so Adam and Eve lived happily, as though the dream had never occurred, until one day, while wandering far east of Eden, Adam discovered a large island shaped like the letter *J*. One of Adam's greatest pleasures was naming things and places, so when he climbed the island's highest mountain, he exclaimed, "Let this be Mount Fuji." Exhilarated by the view from Fuji's summit, Adam gazed down into the valley.

"I am truly happy," he said to himself.

But at that very moment, Adam received a shock. Was that smoke? Could it be? Adam squinted. Were those two human forms? Adam pulled out his pocket Bible and reread the first chapter. Then he squinted again and stealthily descended the mountain to get a better look. Behind a huge rock, Adam trembled. Less than a hundred yards away was another human couple.

With fear, Adam whispered, "Let them be couple J."

Adam eavesdropped, and what he heard struck terror into his heart. Couple J had somehow obtained tractor instructions and was contemplating the same decision: to save or not to save. To his horror, Adam overheard the decision: couple J would save enough for not one but two tractors. When darkness fell, Adam fled the island and raced to Eden to report the news. An agitated discussion ensued.

"We should ignore what the J's do," said Eve firmly. "We made our decision. Let them make theirs. If they are willing to make the present sacrifice, let them enjoy a higher standard of living in the future."

As the first economist, Eve pointed out that her subjective "utility" (satisfaction) should depend only on her own (and Adam's) consumption, not on the J's consumption. In fact, she planned to write a standard economics textbook postulating that a person's utility depends only on his own consumption, not on anyone else's.

"Relativity has no place in standard economics," she insisted.

But Adam was not so sure. He said, "This may be a bad time to bring it up, my love, but do we plan to have children? Because if we do, we're going to have a problem. Our children are bound to learn about couple J's children. After all, communication and transportation are bound to improve, and the J's may even come to Eden as tourists. What will we tell our children when they discover that they consume less than J children because we sacrificed less than J parents?"

"We'll tell them," Eve replied adamantly, "that they should avoid standard of living comparisons. We'll teach them that envy is wrong. If all else fails, we'll show them that standard economics textbooks postulate that individuals are unaffected by relativity."

But even as she spoke these words, Eve began to feel uneasy. She was a good economist who had mastered the standard framework, but she retained an open mind about its assumptions.

"What if relativity does matter to our children?" she asked herself. "What if human nature cannot be purged of relativity?"

Adam continued, "There is a certain irony in the confession I'm about to make, but I've been reading some works in evolutionary biology. The argument goes like this. Suppose an individual who monitors his relative position and adjusts his effort accordingly—intensifying it when he's falling behind, relaxing it when he's ahead—is more likely to survive when a crisis, such as famine or predator attack, occurs. If so, then a relativity emotion may be selected for by, dare I say it, a Darwinian process. We may be unable to purge our descendants of relativity. If their standard of living is worse than the J's, they will be unable to ignore it, no matter what we say."

Now it was Eve's turn to be glum. "Maybe we'd better match the J's saving," she said.

Eve's Dream

That night it was Eve's turn to dream. In her dream, she envisioned herself on Mount Fuji, watching the J's below. How they sacrificed in the year the tractors were built! They cut their consumption to $20, saved $80, and built two tractors worth $40 each. But then Eve watched them, the next year, use the two tractors to plant, plow, and harvest. The J's and their children now enjoyed much more than $100 of consumption, and would do so forever. And the additional consumption was not simply food. Somehow, the J's were making and consuming dazzling appliances, undreamed of in Eden.

"No!" Eve cried in her dream. To Eve's horror, she saw the J's board an airplane and travel to Eden. With them they brought their appliances, not for sale, but for show. The children of Eden were filled with awe and wonder. "Why don't we have those?" they asked. Eve saw an expression of sorrow come over the J's faces. They pitied the poor children of Eden.

"No!" Eve screamed, and she awoke, drenched in perspiration. "We can't let it happen. We can't let the J's move ahead of us," she cried. The morning sun had just risen over the horizon.

"Everything has changed," Adam said grimly. "Woe, that I ever set eyes on the J island."

APPENDIX

There's Just No Substitute for Our Own Saving

Resolving to match the J's, Adam and Eve fell into a deep sleep. In the morning, Adam awoke and suddenly exclaimed with joy, "We don't have to save! We don't have to save!"

"What do you mean?" asked Eve sleepily.

"We can borrow from the J's to finance a tractor! If we borrow, we can have our tractor, and we won't have to cut our consumption below $100 in the year we acquire it!"

"So," said Eve, "you think that our solution is simply to borrow from J-land?"

"Well, isn't it?" asked Adam, suddenly growing worried.

"Poor dear," said Eve. "Adam, my love, sit down and have some breakfast. This is one lecture you don't want to hear on an empty stomach."

Adam ate nervously, and then Eve began.

"Suppose that the quantity and quality of land and labor are the same in Eden and J-land. But suppose we save nothing this year, and the J's save for two tractors. If our two economies were isolated, then beginning next year, obviously two tractors would operate in J-land, and none in Eden, so J-land's output would be greater than Eden's.

"But," continued Eve, "suppose our two economies interact. Then I will show you, in a moment, why one of the two tractors would be invested in Eden. In fact, in future years, output in J-land and Eden would be identical, because both economies would have one tractor."

"Yes!" shouted Adam. "That's what I was hoping!"

"Adam, my love, don't celebrate too soon. Let me continue. Remember we said that the rate of return on one tractor would be 50 percent, because it costs $40, but raises output $20 per year. Well, that's true whether it operates in J-land or Eden. But if a second tractor is used in J-land, then the return on the second will be less—for example, 40 percent."

"Why?" asked Adam.

"The reason, Adam, is simple. The first tractor will work the best land in J-land. If a second tractor also operates in J-land, it will work land that is not quite as fertile, so its return will be less. I call this phenomenon *diminishing returns*—remind me to emphasize it when I write my economics textbook.

"But," Eve continued, "if the second tractor is used in Eden, we'll use it to work our best land, and its return will be 50 percent. So if the second tractor is invested in Eden, instead of J-land, it will yield a higher return—50 percent instead of 40 percent. Now, Adam, suppose for a moment you were the J's, and you were willing to save $80. Would you use your $80 to finance two tractors in J-land? Or would you use your $80 to finance one tractor in J-land and one in Eden?"

"Why, the answer is obvious even to me," exclaimed Adam. "I'd split my $80 between one tractor in each country, because then each $40 would earn a 50 percent return. If I put all $80 into tractors in J-land, the first $40 would earn a 50 percent return, but the second $40 would only earn a 40 percent return."

"I'm proud of you," said Eve. "To obtain the higher return, the J's will lend us $40 to obtain one tractor for use in Eden. Thus, in future years, both economies will operate with one tractor, and use it to work its best land, so our output and J-land's will be identical."

"But," Adam said, "I'm still shaky on the mechanics of how saving in J-land finances investment in Eden."

"Of course," replied Eve patiently. "Let's elaborate our ritual."

She led Adam to the two boulders and reminded him that one was a bank.

"This bank," Eve explained, "would receive all saving, and lend it to investors to purchase tractors. In the year when saving and investment occur, both economies produce $100 of output and income. We save nothing, and the J's save $80—enough to finance two tractors, $40 each. The J's bring $80 of saving to the bank. The bank lends it out to whoever can use it to generate the highest return."

"Why does the bank care about who can generate the highest return?" asked Adam.

"Because, my love," Eve replied, "the bank will charge interest on the loan to the borrowers, and the higher the return on the investment, the higher the interest the bank can collect. The J savers, of course, will ultimately receive this interest.

"Now, " Eve continued, "imagine that you and I go to the bank as investors seeking to borrow $40 to buy a tractor, and J investors with the same motive come to the bank as well. On the first tractor, we and the J's will each generate a 50 percent return. Then the bank can charge us interest of just under 50 percent, and we will still find it worth borrowing, because the return on the tractor will slightly exceed the interest we must pay the bank. But J investors who seek a second tractor will find the interest rate too high, because they can generate only a 40 percent return on the second tractor. So we will get the loan, not them."

"I feel sorry for the J's," Adam laughed. "We save nothing, they save $80 for two tractors, and yet one tractor gets invested and used in both economies, so that we can produce the same output as they can in future years. Thrift is folly."

"Ah, Adam, I'm afraid you've missed the crucial point. Let's go a step further. Just as the tractor is 'permanent' and never wears out (recall that God has not yet cursed mankind with depreciation), so that a $40 tractor raises output by $20 in every future year, let's assume that the bank is willing to give us a permanent loan so that we never have to repay the principal—the $40—but must pay a constant amount of interest in every future year. Having permanently borrowed $40, in each future year we will owe the bank nearly $20 per year of interest, because the bank's interest rate is just under 50 percent. Who do you think will ultimately receive this interest? The J's, who saved in the initial year. In all future years, interest payments will flow from Eden to J-land through the bank.

"Let's suppose," Eve continued, "that there is no further saving by anyone in future years. Both economies will produce the same output—$120 per year of food—because the $40 tractor has raised output from $100 to $120 in both economies. But although one tractor is used in each economy, in effect the J's own both tractors. Because of their saving in the initial year, they receive the return from both tractors. Thus, we will continue to consume only $100, because we must pay $20 of interest to the J's, through the bank, while the J's will consume $140 per year— the $120 they produce in J-land, plus the $20 they can buy with our interest payments."

At last Adam seemed to follow Eve's analysis. "If someone looked at our two economies in future years," he said, "they might think we have the same standard of living because we each use one tractor, so our machinery per worker is the same, and our output per worker—our labor productivity—is the same. But they would be mistaken."

"Exactly right," said Eve. "What counts is who owns the capital equipment—the tractors. The J's own both tractors even though each economy uses one in production. Thus, the J's have a *wealth* of $80, and we have no wealth. As a result, the J's wealth generates $40 of capital income, a 50 percent return on their wealth. Both we and the J's earn $100 of labor income, but the J's earn $40 of capital income. Thus, the J's total income is $140 while ours is $100, and in future years, their consumption will be $140, while ours will be $100."

Eve continued. "Wealth is *net worth*. We possess $40 of assets—one tractor—but our liabilities are also $40 because we borrowed $40 from J-land; so our net worth (assets minus liabilities) is zero. By contrast, the J's net worth is $80. They possess a $40 tractor, and they are also owed $40 by us. In fact, we will give them a $40 Eden bond to hold to indicate this, so their total assets are $80. With zero liabilities, their net worth is $80. Hence, our wealth is zero, and theirs is $80. And the difference in wealth is, of course, due to the difference in saving."

"So," continued Adam, "we would be in debt to J-land. We would be a debtor nation, because our wealth—zero—would be less than our capital stock—$40. And J-land would be a creditor nation, because its wealth—$80—would exceed its own capital stock—$40. So every year, debtor nation Eden would make interest payments of $20 to creditor nation J-land."

"That's right," replied Eve.

"Then," concluded Adam, "what matters for our future standard of living is the saving we do, not the investment that occurs within our borders."

"I'm proud of you," exclaimed Eve. "Suppose we tried to ignore the fact that the J's saved $80 and we saved nothing. We might try to defend ourselves by pointing out that investment was $40 in both economies. Each country obtained one tractor. Then, in future years, we could point out that both economies produced $120 of output. But, in fact, their standard of living would be higher, because they would have more wealth, receive interest payments from us, and therefore would afford more consumption."

"I have one last question," said Adam with new confidence. "One $40 tractor raises output $20 per year—a 50 percent return. You assumed that the J savers will capture the full return, so we will pay them a 50 percent interest rate, or $20 per year. But isn't it possible they will capture only a fraction of the 50 percent return, and we will capture a fraction ourselves? For example, maybe we will only pay them 25 percent (not 50 percent) of $40, or $10 per year, and keep $10 per year for ourselves."

"I have a confession," said Eve. "You are right. If the tractor raises the *marginal* product of our labor or land (the increase in output due to the last unit of labor or land), then we will capture a fraction of the return, so the outcome won't be so bad. I'll explain why, any day you are willing to hear a lecture on the marginal productivity theory of income distribution.

"But," continued Eve, "my simplification is justified because it doesn't change the basic point. If they save and we don't, then even if the J's capture only a fraction of the full return, their future standard of living will still exceed ours. The reason is simple. The J's, who own all labor, land, and capital used in J-land, will obviously capture the full return on the $40 tractor invested in J-land. And as long as J savers capture some of the return on the $40 tractor invested in Eden, we will capture only a fraction of the full return. So due to the two tractors, the J's future standard of living must be higher than ours, even if we capture a fraction of the return on our $40 tractor."

Adam looked glum. Finally, he said, "Eve, I understand that if the J's save and we don't, they'll live better than we will because we'll pay them interest every year. But exactly how would they get more of our crop to consume? What would happen to exports and imports?"

"Let's trace it through," said Eve. "In the year of saving and investment, assume one tractor is built in each economy, so each economy produces $60 of food, and a $40 tractor. But we borrow $40 from J savers through the bank. We use the $40 to keep our consumption at $100, while the J's reduce their consumption to $20, saving $80 of their income. Clearly, we must import $40 of food from J-land to keep our consumption of food at $100, and the J's would export $40 of food and consume only $20 of food."

"So," said Adam, "in that first year we would run a trade deficit of $40, and J-land would run a trade surplus of $40."

"But," said Eve, "let's now consider each future year. Both economies produce $120 of food, but we consume $100, and the J's consume $140. Clearly, we must export $20 of food to J-land. So in each future year, we would run a trade surplus of $20, and J-land would run a trade deficit of $20. Yet they would have the higher standard of living."

"But the trade balance leaves out something important," exclaimed Adam. "It includes only payments from the flow of goods—$20 of food. But while we're receiving $20 from the J's for food, we're paying $20 to the J's for interest on the original $40 loan. Every year, the J's use the $20 of interest they receive from us to buy $20 of food from us."

"Adam, that's impressive reasoning," smiled Eve. "You're right. We do need a balance that includes interest payments as well as payments for goods. I propose we call it the *current account* balance. In each future year, our current account balance would be zero, because our receipts from $20 of food would be offset by our $20 of interest payments."

"But," sighed Adam, "even though our current account balance would be zero, and our trade balance would be a surplus of $20, our standard of living would be lower than J-land's."

"Exactly right," said Eve with a smile.

"So," said Adam, "it would be a mistake for us to feel good about our current account balance of zero and our trade surplus of $20, because what really matters is that the J's would be enjoying a higher standard of living, since they had saved and accumulated more wealth. So even if the headlines focus on the trade and current account balances, the most important thing to watch is who is saving more and accumulating more wealth, because that's what clearly tells who will enjoy the higher standard of living in the future."

"Adam," said Eve with obvious affection and tears in her eyes, "you've made me truly happy. You've grasped some basic economics."

Adam and Eve went outside, and stood silently looking at the far eastern horizon where they could see the snowy peak of Mount Fuji faintly in the distance.

"I pledge to you, Eve, that we will save enough to finance not one, but two tractors. We will match the J's in wealth accumulation. Our children's standard of living will be second to none in the world."

Together, Adam and Eve walked bravely toward the sunrise.

2 RAISE THE NATIONAL SAVING RATE

Senator Myopia had the Mall crowd cheering. Outside, the snow fell, and a weaker people might have huddled in their homes. But undaunted, sturdy Americans had ventured out into the winter storm, lured by the warmth of the great American Mall. Now in the warm belly of the Mall, surrounded by sparkling shop windows, how glad they were that their pioneer fortitude had triumphed.

The shop windows of the great American Mall vibrated as the crowd roared its approval. Only a speaker like Senator Myopia could grab the attention of frantic Mall shoppers and interrupt their frenzied purchases.

"I'm sick and tired of the party poopers, the killjoys, the austerity pushers, and the discipline devotees who say we must sacrifice to stay number one. How dare they attack our most sacred institution, the great American Mall!" roared Senator Myopia.

"You know, I've traced my lineage all the way back to ancient Greece and Rome, but my fellow Americans, let me tell you something. The Romans were great builders, but their empire fell, and do you know why? Because they never built a great Mall. And this, my friends, is why America shall endure and thrive forever. Oh sure, we must save more. Sure, we must invest more. But first and foremost, my fellow Americans, we must consume more!" The crowd erupted in thunderous applause.

"Let's make those cash registers hum," continued the senator. "The more we consume, the stronger our economy will be. Who dares to spoil our party?" mocked the senator as the crowd broke into approving laughter.

"I do," said a young man in the corner. The crowd hushed, and a thousand eyes turned to him. He began to speak, but Senator Myopia immediately interrupted him.

"So you'd like to spoil our party, would you?" asked Senator Myopia with a confident grin. "And you expect us to listen to you. But just look at you. Your clothes. Who handed them down to you, your older brother or your father?" The crowd began to snicker.

"And there's nothing in your arms, except a single book. Where are your packages? Could it be you left your credit cards home? Or don't you even have a set of credit cards?" The very thought of someone without credit cards sent the crowd into a fit of laughter.

But the young man seemed unruffled. In a calm voice he said: "In order to raise our saving rate, we must reduce our consumption rate. If our saving rate is 20 percent, our consumption rate is 80 percent. Raising the saving rate from 20 percent to 24 percent means reducing the consumption rate from 80 percent to 76 percent."

Now Senator Myopia became angry. "That's the stupidest thing I've ever heard. I say we can raise both our saving rate and our consumption rate at the same time."

"I'm afraid that's not possible, Senator," the young man continued. "You see, saving is defined as income minus consumption. The saving rate is the fraction of income saved, and the consumption rate is the fraction of income consumed. The two must add up to 100 percent. So if the saving rate is to go up, the consumption rate must go down. I'm afraid it's that simple."

"Who are you?" shouted the angry senator. "What do you do for a living?" muttered voices in the crowd.

"I'm an economist," answered the young man in a quiet voice.

"An economist!" Senator Myopia smirked. "Did you hear that, my fellow Americans? An economist! Is this the kind of person you would invite to your house for dinner? Would you want your children around this kind of person? What do you do for fun, young man, read a textbook?" The crowd went wild with derisive laughter.

"Ignore him, Senator!" shouted the crowd. And so the senator did. He brought his oration to a dramatic crescendo.

"Consume, consume, consume, my fellow Americans. Let's go out and spend ourselves rich!" With that, the crowd cheered and burst into the waiting shops. The senator and his party soon left, triumphant.

But in the corner, the young man remained. And he did not remain alone. Several people, young and old, quietly gathered around him, and urged him to teach them. And here is what he said.

Capital Accumulation

I'm afraid, my friends, I've begun with a simple, unpleasant truth. A higher saving rate inescapably means a lower consumption rate. So, should we raise the saving rate? Yes, I believe there is a decisive reason for raising our saving rate: the relative standard of living of our children and grandchildren. If we do not raise our saving rate, then within a few decades, several other nations will overtake our standard of living. If we maintain our current saving rate, today we will enjoy the highest consumption per person in the world, but tomorrow our children and grandchildren will not.

Senator Myopia mocked my clothes. He accused me of not caring about consumption. But that is untrue. I do not come to preach against materialism. Far from it. I love stereos, airplane travel, and many other material things. I do not place myself above my fellow citizens who shop frantically all around us. My difference with Senator Myopia is simply this: In his obsession with consumption today, he forgets about consumption tomorrow. He fails to grasp what we must do today to protect consumption tomorrow. He thinks the best way to achieve high consumption tomorrow is to enjoy fast consumption growth today. Unfortunately, he is wrong. So I come to plead for a higher saving rate today, not because I am against consumption, but because I am for it—in the future as well as the present. I want our future consumption to be second to none in the world.

Nor am I an extremist. I don't advocate an actual cut in our consumption, only slower consumption growth for a few years. Instead of our normal 2.5 percent consumption growth, let it grow 1.5 percent for half a decade. I want a small cut in our consumption *rate* (the fraction of our output that we consume) each year for several years—small enough so that our dollar consumption keeps rising each year, yet more slowly than it would otherwise.

To understand my case for gradually raising our national saving rate, you must first understand what capital accumulation is, and how it raises the standard of living (the level of consumption per person).

Let me begin with a question. What determines the rate of improvement in a nation's standard of living in the long run? Of course, many factors influence the rate of advance. But one source, my friends, deserves the spotlight: capital accumulation. What is capital accumulation? Are you thinking of stocks and bonds, those impressive pieces of paper we often lock up in a bank vault for safety? Or are you thinking of financial capital, the funds that finance the purchase of stocks and bonds? By "capital," I do not mean either the pieces of paper or the funds that buy them. Instead, I mean *real* capital, which, when combined with labor, produces real output. Capital enables the average worker to produce more output.

What do you think real capital is? Are you thinking of machines? Many people think capital consists solely of physical capital, like machines. But this view of capital is too narrow. Of course, physical capital is vital. What would our standard of living be without machinery, factories, roads, and bridges? Where would today's farmer be without a tractor?

But capital is more than machinery. Capital is also the stock of technical knowledge accumulated from past experience. This stock of "blueprints" tells us how to produce specific goods and services. Just imagine the consequence of a national amnesia that would require us to reinvent the wheel and everything else. Did you realize that capital is also the skill of the labor force that is acquired by education and training? The stock of blueprints and machinery are not very effective unless the workforce has accumulated the human capital (skills) needed to follow the blueprints and operate the machines.

Suppose the capital stock is $2,000 billion on January 1 and that during the year $500 billion of new capital goods are produced and $300 billion of old capital goods wear out—*depreciate*—so that the capital stock is $2,200 billion on December 31. Then we say that this year's *gross investment is* $500 billion and *net investment is* $200 billion. So *net* investment is the net increase in the capital stock that occurs during the year—in this example, $200 billion. In a given year, capital accumulation equals net investment.

Now imagine a simple economy that produces only two goods: corn, the consumption (C) good; and tractors, the investment (I) good. Assume that all available labor, capital, and land will be utilized to produce either corn or tractors. The economic year is beginning. How much labor, capital, and land will be assigned to make tractors, and how much to make corn? Clearly, more labor, capital, and land for tractors means less labor, capital, and land for corn. The tractor production sector—the I sector—can only expand if the corn production sector—the C sector—contracts.

How nice to imagine a world with only corn and tractors. But let's return to the real economy. What belongs in the C sector? The I sector? Obviously, a wheat farm is in the C sector, and a tractor factory is in the I sector. But what about a school? A school should also be in the I sector because it produces human capital. So should the research and development division of every business firm, because the division produces knowledge capital. Capital accumulation increases when a greater share of production occurs in the I sector, and less in the C sector.

Each unit of input—land, labor, or capital—can be assigned to produce goods and services that will be used up—consumed—this year, or to produce goods and services that raise the productive power of workers in the future. The more units of input that are assigned to produce C goods, the fewer that are available to produce I goods.

Imagine a circular pie, representing national output, that is divided into two unequal parts. The large slice is consumption, and the small slice is investment. The only way to increase the investment slice is to reduce the consumption slice. A higher investment rate (percentage) requires a lower consumption rate (percentage). If more land, labor, and capital are devoted to the production of investment goods, less must be allocated to the production of consumer goods.

So I'm afraid we can't escape a painful truth, no matter what Senator Myopia says. Capital accumulation requires a sacrifice in the present. In order to build machinery (physical capital), improve our skills (human capital), or invent new technology (knowledge capital), time and resources must be diverted away from producing goods and services for current consumption. But does capital accumulation really raise future *productivity* (output per worker)? Let's use some common sense. Why is the productivity of the average American worker today so much higher than the productivity of the average American worker one hundred years ago? Is it because our great-grandparents were lazy, and we work hard? Nonsense.

The central reason is that today's American worker has more education and skill (human capital), utilizes more and better machinery and technology (physical capital), and follows a more advanced set of blueprints (knowledge capital).

Compare the primitive farmer, who lacks both a tractor and the skill to operate it, with the modern farmer, who possesses both the tractor (physical capital) and the ability to operate it (human capital). Moreover, the modern farmer utilizes knowledge capital accumulated from past experience, research, and invention to tell him which farming techniques will be most productive. Is it any wonder that output per worker—productivity—is much higher for the modern farmer?

Countless urban and industrial as well as rural examples make the commonsense point: Raising capital per worker generally raises output per worker. Raising capital per worker is therefore the key to raising the standard of living, or consumption per person.

So far I have said nothing about saving. I have explained why capital accumulation through investment is the key to advancing the standard of living, and why raising the investment rate requires reducing the consumption rate. But what about saving? More investment requires more saving, for the simple reason that investment must equal saving. Why?

Saving is defined as income not consumed. Investment is defined as output not consumed. But income must equal output, because for every dollar of output sold, a dollar of income is earned. If output and income are $1,000 billion, and consumption is $900 billion, then income not consumed—saving—is $100 billion; and output not consumed—investment—is also $100 billion.

Keep this simple example in mind. To finance the $100 billion of investment—the purchase of machinery—imagine that business firms issue $100 billion of bonds, and savers purchase the $100 billion of bonds. In effect, business firms borrow $100 billion from savers (lenders) to invest in $100 billion worth of machinery. The machinery generates a real return—it raises output. Firms use the additional revenue earned on the machinery to pay interest to savers (bondholders). In this example, we can say that the $100 billion of saving is necessary to *finance* the $100 billion of investment. National income is $1,000 billion. Households choose to consume 90 percent ($900 billion) and save 10 percent ($100 billion). This saving is what makes possible the $100 billion of investment.

So the only way to raise capital accumulation is to raise saving. Raising the national saving rate—the fraction of national income that is saved rather than consumed—is the key to raising the future standard of living.

The Saving Rate Must Be Raised Gradually

But here we are, surrounded by shop windows displaying consumer goods, and I am claiming that raising our saving rate will raise our future standard of living. How can I claim that? If we raise our saving rate, we reduce our consumption rate. But won't this mean less spending at the Mall? And won't the Mall cut its orders from manufacturers of consumer goods? And won't these manufacturers cut production and lay off workers? Economists call a fall in output and employment a *recession*. So won't the result be a recession?

Yes, there would be a recession if we raised the saving rate suddenly and sharply. But there need be no recession if we raise it gradually. Why?

Here's the key point. Today, output, consumption, and investment all grow at roughly 2.5 percent per year. Our aim is to make consumption grow more slowly—say 1.5 percent per year instead of 2.5 percent—while we make investment grow more rapidly, for about half a decade. If we gradually raise the saving rate, dollar consumption will simply grow more slowly, but it will never actually decline. Thereafter, consumption, investment, and output will all grow somewhat faster than 2.5 percent due to the permanently higher investment rate.

When I say we must reduce the consumption *rate* (the fraction of output that we consume) to raise the investment rate, this doesn't mean that dollar consumption must literally decline from one year to the next. So the Mall will never suffer a decline in sales, only a slower growth in sales.

What will happen if the saving rate is raised gradually, or equivalently, if the consumption rate is reduced gradually? As workers voluntarily quit and retire in the consumption goods (C) sector, they

will not be replaced. Most new jobs will open up in the investment goods (I) sector. So layoffs will be avoided in the C sector.

Of course, if we were foolish and tried to shift the relative size
of the consumption and investment goods sectors too quickly,
then we would need to force workers out of the C sector. The
result would be layoffs. But by raising the saving rate gradually,
we can avoid layoffs. Voluntary job leaving *(quits)* and retire-
ments will handle the required contraction in the C sector's
workforce.

But can we be sure that jobs in the I sector will expand enough
to prevent a rise in unemployment? As the great economist John
Maynard Keynes emphasized in his classic, *The General Theory
of Employment, Interest, and Money* (1936), when household demand for consumer goods grows more slowly, this does not guarantee that business demand for investment goods will grow more
rapidly. But unless it does, the economy will not generate enough
new jobs, and unemployment will rise.

Here is where our central bank, the Federal Reserve ("the
Fed") comes in. It is the Fed's job to make sure that the investment goods sector grows more rapidly when the consumer goods
sector grows more slowly, so that enough new jobs are created in
the economy to prevent unemployment from rising. How can the
Fed do this?

Simple. The Fed can reduce interest rates. When interest rates
fall, business firms throughout the economy are encouraged to
borrow to buy machinery and new technology. They raise their
demand for investment goods. The lower the interest rates, the
greater the demand for investment goods. In turn, the firms making I goods will need more workers to meet the increased demand. So more new jobs will be created in the I sector.

But how does the Fed lower interest rates? By injecting more
money into the economy and the banking system. How? By *open
market operations,* or buying government bonds from households, businesses, or local governments. The sellers of bonds
deposit the money in banks. In response to the infusion of cash
reserves, banks try to increase lending. To attract borrowers for

their excess funds, banks compete by reducing interest rates. At lower interest rates, business firms find it profitable to borrow more to buy more investment goods. So the Fed's action results in an increase in investment demand by business firms.

John Maynard Keynes wrote a brilliant book in the 1930s, but it has been misinterpreted. Many people have come to believe that saving hurts the economy. It is simply not true that an increase in saving must cause a recession. It is only true if the Fed fails to implement routine, appropriate, offsetting monetary policy. Once again, what must the Fed do? When the demand for consumer goods grows more slowly, so few new jobs are created in the C sector, the Fed must make sure that demand for investment goods grows more rapidly so that enough new jobs are created in the I sector. The Fed can easily do this by reducing interest rates, thereby encouraging business firms to borrow to buy more I-sector goods.

But this is all theory. Does it work in practice? Look at other countries. For the past few decades, Japan has had a much higher saving rate than we. So have several European countries. Yet these high-saving countries have not had more recessions, or higher unemployment rates, over these decades. So the theory works in practice. A higher saving rate does not imply a higher unemployment rate.

Let's sum up. If the saving rate is raised gradually, and the Fed earns its pay by implementing proper monetary policy, then our economy can adjust to a higher saving rate without a recession or a rise in unemployment. The higher saving rate means that a larger fraction of our output will be I goods instead of C goods.

So you thought you were helping the economy by consuming? You said, "Who will buy goods, if not us? And if we don't buy goods, producers won't make them. And if they don't make them, workers will be laid off. And there will be hard times. So we are patriots when we consume, and traitors when we save."

But now you see your error. You are guilty of the sin of pride. You consumers are not the only buyers of goods in the economy. Business firms buy goods—investment goods. The correct way to look at it is this: The more consumer goods you demand, the more consumer goods producers will make, and the fewer resources—labor, capital, materials, and land—will be available to make investment goods. So you are directly competing with business firms. More consumer goods for you means fewer investment goods for them.

You thought you were heroes, the only buyers in town. Without you, you thought, nobody would buy goods, production would plummet, and down would go the economy. What pride! But you are not the only buyers in town. Business firms are also buyers. And your buying of consumer goods interferes with their buying of investment goods, because the total output of goods that can be produced in a given year is limited.

So don't flatter yourselves. The economy's health does not depend on fast growth in your consumer spending. If you slow the growth of your consumer spending, the Fed will make sure that business firms quicken the growth of their investment spending, and total spending will still grow normally. But now more of the growth in output will be in investment goods, and less in consumer goods.

So, if some economist sets before you a policy that will encourage saving and discourage consumption, do not tremble for the fate of the economy. Such a policy is exactly what is needed to raise the future productive power of the economy. As long as the policy is phased in gradually, so that it raises the saving rate gradually, do not fear it, but welcome it. Such a policy is economic medicine that is safe and effective.

Senator Myopia's Mistake

But I can hear Senator Myopia. He went around the country blustering, "Who says we can't raise our consumption and investment at the same time? I know how to do it. Let's cut taxes, but don't worry, I won't cut government spending—I don't want to cut your favorite programs. My tax cut will still work, though. If I cut your taxes $100, you'll consume $90 and save $10. More saving means more investment, so we'll get more of both—consumption and investment!"

Was he right? Unfortunately, he was not. But where is the mistake? Let's see if we can find it.

First of all, he was right about one thing: If your taxes are cut, you'll consume more, and if you consume more, then the C-goods sector will raise its production. But he ignored the fact that the C-goods sector will then have to draw labor, capital, and land away from the I-goods sector, so production of I goods will be forced down. More corn means fewer tractors. If taxes are cut $100 billion, and households consume $90 billion more, then the I sector will be forced to produce $90 billion less.

True, if taxes are cut $100 billion, households might raise their saving $10 billion. Doesn't more saving mean more investment? Didn't I say earlier that saving equals investment? So where is the mistake?

Yes, *national* saving must equal national investment. But national saving is the sum of household, business, and government saving. The tax cut will raise household saving. In fact, in our example, households save 10 percent of the tax cut, or $10 billion. The mistake is forgetting about the impact of the tax cut on another component of national saving—government saving.

What is government saving? Saving is always income minus consumption. Therefore, government saving is government net income minus government consumption. Government net income equals tax revenue minus cash "transfer" payments to households or business firms, such as Social Security benefit payments. Government consumption is the purchase of goods or services by government that yields current rather than future benefits to citizens—for example, the purchase of the labor services of recreation workers on public playgrounds. Actually, most government purchases are investment rather than consumption because the goods and services yield future rather than current benefits. For example, the purchase of labor services for the construction of highways or schools, or the purchase of military goods such as tanks, yields benefits primarily in the future. So government saving is determined mainly by government net income—taxes minus transfers.

Now that we have the spotlight on government saving, we can illuminate Senator Myopia's error. Senator Myopia is holding government spending constant; he wants you to have all your favorite programs, including transfers and government consumption. So what happens to government saving when taxes are cut $100 billion while government spending is held constant? While households cheer the $100 billion tax cut, the poor government treasurer is despondent: government net income falls $100 billion, and since government consumption stays constant, government saving falls $100 billion.

Since household saving increases $10 billion but government saving falls $100 billion, national saving falls $90 billion. So national investment must also fall $90 billion. And this is exactly the same answer we obtained before by recognizing that consumption would increase $90 billion, forcing investment down $90 billion.

Then what is Senator Myopia's mistake? He forgets that household saving is not the same thing as national saving. A $100 billion tax cut may raise household saving $10 billion, but it reduces national saving $90 billion, and therefore, reduces national investment $90 billion.

Am I claiming that any tax cut must reduce national saving? Not at all. Senator Myopia overlooked one little detail. He forgot to match his tax cut with an equal cut in government transfer spending. What would have happened if the $100 billion tax cut were matched by a $100 billion cut in government transfer spending?

The answer is simple. There would have been no change in national saving. Taxpayers would have consumed $90 billion more, but transfer recipients would have consumed $90 billion less, so there would have been no change in total consumption. Taxpayers would have saved $10 billion more, but transfer recipients would have saved $10 billion less. Government net income—taxes minus transfers—would have been unchanged, so there would have been no change in national saving.

Thus, an equal cut in taxes and government transfers has no effect on national saving and investment. What hurts national saving and investment, however, is a tax cut that is not matched by an equal cut in government transfer spending. Shame on you, Senator Myopia.

Old Karl's Mistake

We can learn about the importance of capital accumulation from history. Why did the average American in the 1920s have a much higher standard of living than the average American in the 1820s? Why is the average American of the 1990s much better off than the average American of the 1920s? Why was poverty the rule two hundred years ago, but the exception today in the United States? For that matter, why is it the rule today in some countries, but the exception in others?

A dramatic story in the ascent of man began some two hundred years ago: the Industrial Revolution. Today, with hindsight, it is clear that it eventually resulted in a drastic reduction in poverty. But we would do well to remind ourselves that the early reactions were, to put it mildly, mixed. The Luddites did not exactly welcome machinery. And with good reason. Here were profit-driven entrepreneurs replacing people with machines. Machines were not poverty reducers, said the Luddites; they were poverty creators. Where would it lead? Greedy capitalists would keep substituting capital for labor. Unemployment would rise, and workers would be impoverished. Incidentally, the same argument was made about automation in the 1960s. And many believe it today.

There is one little problem with this logic. How is it that today, with so much more machinery per person, the unemployment rate is no higher than two hundred years ago, and the average worker is so much better off? There must be a flaw in the logic. What is it?

Here's the mistake. The Luddite argument really says this: "If you're going to produce the same output but now use more machines, then you're going to need less labor." Correct. But who says we're going to produce the same output? Suppose instead that we add machines, but keep the same labor. Then we'll get more output. And that is, in fact, what happened over the long run for the economy as a whole.

Of course, it didn't always happen in the short run at a particular factory, which is how the argument got started that machinery impoverishes workers. In the short run, the workers at a particular plant were not dreaming. Some really were laid off because of the introduction of machinery. Why? Why couldn't the employer simply keep all the workers and raise output? Because in the short run, the market for this particular product may not have supported so large an increase in its output. So in some cases, the introduction of machinery did cause layoffs. And workers were unemployed until they could find jobs elsewhere.

To understand why it all worked out well in the end, let's consider the argument of someone who is still remembered today for predicting otherwise: good old Karl Marx. Many people think that old Karl disputed every claim made by advocates of capitalism. But this is untrue. He only took issue with the last claim: that eventually capitalism would pull workers out of poverty.

Marx fully agreed that machinery raises the productivity of workers—output per person. He conceded that profits were often saved, that saving financed investment in machinery, that machinery increased the output of each worker, and that this could *potentially* enable the capitalist to raise the wage, and hence consumption, of the average worker. But Marx denied that the wage would in fact be raised enough to enable workers to escape poverty.

Instead, he contended that the greedy capitalists would hold down the wage despite the worker's higher productivity. To be fair to old Karl, he may have conceded that some rise in the absolute wage might occur. But he insisted that the wage of workers would deteriorate relatively if not absolutely. The failure of the wage to keep pace with worker productivity would, Marx predicted, lead to less than complete happiness among the masses. You know the rest. Now at certain times and places, old

Karl was right. The rise in worker productivity, made possible by machinery, was not matched by a comparable rise in the wage. But over the long haul, it is now clear that it would be hard to make a more inaccurate prediction. In fact, the real wage and consumption of today's worker in capitalist economies is dramatically higher than it was 150 years ago. The rise in worker productivity has eventually led to a significant rise in the worker's wage and standard of living.

So how did this happen? Why did the worker's wage eventually rise with his productivity? Most economists, myself included, give the following answer.

Imagine you're a profit-seeking employer back in the good old days. How do you decide how many workers to hire? Figure out the additional output, and hence additional revenue, that another worker will give you. Compare it to the wage you must pay him. If the additional revenue exceeds the additional cost, hire him, and make the same comparison for the next worker. Of course, as diminishing returns sets in, it eventually does not pay to hire any more at the going wage. Suppose, like a good profit-seeking capitalist, you decide to stop at the hundredth worker, because he adds only slightly more than $1 of revenue per hour, and the going hourly wage is $1.

Now you save some of your profit and use it to invest in new machinery, which raises the productivity of your workers. Suppose that the revenue you obtain from your hundredth worker is now $2, instead of $1. In fact, you calculate that, with your new machinery, you could hire another twenty workers (for a total of 120) before diminishing returns makes another worker's revenue fall to $1.

What do you do? If the going wage is still $1, you try to hire twenty more workers. But now comes a key part of the argument. Assume that there are many other capitalists, and they are doing the same thing you are, so they all want to hire more workers, but most workers are already employed. With only so many workers available, you can't all get what you want. At a $1 wage, the total demand for labor in the economy now exceeds the total supply. So what do you do?

Naturally, you try to bid workers away from other capitalists. You do it by offering a wage slightly above $1, say $1.10. When other workers hear of your offer, some are glad to switch. Of course, other capitalists will not sit idly by and watch their workforce, and profit, disappear. Because they too have introduced machinery, they too will find it profitable to match you, and even raise you. They may raise their wage offer to $1.20, not only winning back their workers, but luring a few of yours. So now what do you do?

Remember, if necessary, you can go all the way to $2 to try to keep your original hundred workers, because your machinery has doubled the productivity of your hundredth worker. But you really don't want to do this. You would like to get all capitalists together in a room and make a speech: "Let's not engage in a foolish wage competition. Where will it get us? Let's keep the wage at $1, be satisfied with the same workforce, and enjoy a nice profit."

But you are a practical capitalist, and you realize that your speech won't work. Why? Because whoever cheats and offers a slightly higher wage will reap even more profit. Every capitalist will realize this, and everyone will be tempted to cheat. If you are foolish enough to hold the line on wages, you will simply lose your workforce and all your profit. Besides, suppose some capitalist is caught cheating. What can you do to him? Expel him from the local capitalist society? He will laugh all the way to the bank.

So you've got no choice. You've got to engage in a wage competition to hold on to your workforce. So sure enough, the wage goes to $1.10, $1.20, and eventually nears $2. There it stops, because at that wage, finally, the typical capitalist does not want to expand his workforce. For example, in your case, your hundredth worker adds revenue of just $2, so it wouldn't pay you to hire more than a hundred if the wage hits $2. So when the wage reaches $2, total demand for labor again matches its supply, and the wage stops rising.

You and the other capitalists shake your heads and mutter,

"What a shame. Oh, if only we could have kept the wage at $1, just like good old Karl said we would." You and other capitalists will probably curl up at the fireplace with a copy of good old Karl's *Das Kapital* and try to console yourselves with the story of what was supposed to happen to the wage.

Now notice a key feature of the economist's explanation. It does not, in any way, assume that the wage rises because capitalists abandon, or even moderate, profit seeking. Just the opposite. The argument assumes that capitalists are motivated solely by profit seeking. But it is exactly this profit seeking that makes an agreement against wage competition impractical. Sure, it would be better for all capitalists if they all stuck to the agreement. But whoever breaks it first will make even more profit in the short run. And so, with many capitalists, the agreement simply won't hold.

Of course, few economists insist that this explanation is the whole story. Sure, there were probably some capitalists who thought their workers deserved a wage increase. And there were no doubt many who liked everything about *Das Kapital* except the ending, and who therefore concluded that it might be prudent for all capitalists to raise wages. And of course, trade unions certainly played a role in raising wages at particular workplaces.

But the economist's central point is this: As long as each capitalist cares enough about his own profit to engage in wage competition, the wage will rise with productivity. So whatever raises productivity will raise the worker's wage, and reduce poverty. And it is capital accumulation that raises productivity. So capital accumulation has long been a vital engine for reducing poverty. It is time to recognize this fact in our public discussion.

The United States Is a Low-Saving Country by International Standards

Where do we stand internationally when it comes to saving? Near the bottom, I'm afraid. Table 2.1 shows gross saving as a percentage of gross domestic product (GDP) for the Organization

Table 2.1

Gross Saving as a Percentage of GDP

	1960s		1970s		1980s		1990–92	
	Rank & %		Rank & %		Rank & %		Rank & %	
Japan	1	34.5	1	35.3	1	31.7	1	34.3
Switzerland	2	29.4	2	28.6	2	28.5	2	30.2
Norway	6	27.4	4	26.8	3	27.7	7	23.5
Austria	4	27.7	3	28.0	4	24.3	4	25.8
Portugal	15	23.1	6	26.0	5	24.3	3	25.9
Finland	9	25.4	5	26.7	6	24.2	17	17.3
Netherlands	5	27.6	11	24.9	7	23.1	6	24.9
Germany	7	27.3	13	24.3	8	22.3	8	23.5
Italy	3	28.1	7	25.9	9	22.0	13	18.7
Spain	11	24.7	10	25.5	10	21.1	10	20.9
Canada	17	21.9	16	22.9	11	20.7	19	15.4
Australia	12	24.7	14	24.1	12	20.6	16	17.9
France	8	26.2	8	25.8	13	20.5	11	20.7
New Zealand	18	21.2	17	22.2	14	20.1	15	18.1
Turkey	23	14.8	23	17.1	15	19.3	12	19.8
Iceland	10	25.4	12	24.8	16	18.7	20	15.4
Ireland	21	18.4	18	21.3	17	18.4	5	25.0
United States	**19**	**19.9**	**21**	**19.6**	**18**	**17.7**	**21**	**15.1**
Greece	20	19.2	9	25.8	19	17.7	22	14.9
Sweden	13	24.0	19	21.1	20	17.7	18	16.5
Belgium	16	22.4	15	23.1	21	16.9	9	21.3
United Kingdom	22	18.4	22	17.9	22	16.6	23	13.8
Denmark	14	23.3	20	20.9	23	15.4	14	18.6

Source: OECD, *Taxation and Household Savings,* Table 2.1, pp. 21–24 (Paris, 1994).

for Economic Cooperation and Development (OECD) countries for the 1960s, 1970s, and 1980s, and from 1990 to 1992. Recall that GDP is the total output produced in the country. Gross saving includes the gross saving of households, firms, and government. Of the twenty-three OECD countries, the United States ranked nineteenth in the 1960s, twenty-first in the 1970s, eighteenth in the 1980s, and twenty-first in the first three years of the 1990s. While the leaders of the 1980s, Japan and Switzerland, saved 31.7 percent and 28.5 percent, respectively, the United States managed to save only 17.7 percent.

Table 2.2

Net Saving as a Percentage of Net National Income (in %)

	1970s	1980s	1990–92
Japan	25.6	20.9	23.0
Germany	15.1	11.2	12.4
France	17.1	9.0	8.7
Italy	16.4	11.2	7.6
United States	**9.1**	**5.2**	**2.5**
OECD	13.8	9.7	8.7

Source: OECD, *National Accounts 1960–1992, Main Aggregates, Volume I* (Paris, 1994); percentages computed by the author.

Table 2.2 shows net saving as a percentage of net national income for the five OECD countries with the largest GDPs in 1992. Net saving equals gross saving minus depreciation of the capital stock; hence, net saving indicates the saving in excess of what is required merely to offset depreciation. Positive net saving is necessary to actually increase the capital stock. Net national income equals gross national income minus depreciation.

Of the five largest (by GDP) OECD countries, the United States had the smallest net saving rate in all three decades by a wide margin, well below the average of all OECD countries. The net saving rate of all five countries (and the whole OECD) declined from the 1970s to the 1980s; however, in the early 1990s, Japan and Germany halted their decline—Japan at 23.0 percent, Germany at 12.4 percent—while the U.S. net saving rate declined to just 2.5 percent.

The Case for Raising Our Saving Rate

A strong case can be made that our current saving rate is too low. The case has two parts: a traditional economic argument, and a novel economic argument.

We begin with the traditional argument. The current U.S. saving rate is not a free market reflection of our preferences between present and future consumption because of several government interventions that reduce our saving rate. What are these interventions?

We indirectly tax future consumption by taxing capital income (interest, dividends, and capital gains) under the current income tax. Capital income taxes reduce the future consumption that can be obtained from a given amount of saving. The choice between future and present consumption is therefore biased against the future by our income tax.

Another source of distortion is social insurance: Social Security, unemployment insurance, and Medicare. Social Security has made a great contribution to the well-being of the elderly for many decades. But many people surely save less, knowing that Social Security will help out when they retire. Similarly, without unemployment insurance and Medicare, many citizens would save more to prepare for the possibility of being laid off or needing medical care in old age. Thus, government social insurance, while generating great benefits for the citizenry, has almost surely reduced the national saving rate.

A final source of distortion is government saving, one important component of national saving. Government saving is not market-generated, but determined politically by Congress and the president. Politicians may believe it is easier for voters to appreciate a tax cut or benefit increase than to grasp the future gain that will result from government saving.

Now let's turn to the novel economic argument. Any economics text teaches that certain goods are "non-exclusionary": even if someone refuses to pay for the good, we cannot prevent her from benefiting from it. We can exclude you from enjoying a TV if you refuse to pay for it, so a TV is a private good. But if we improve the police protection in your area, we cannot exclude you from benefiting even if you refuse to pay, so police protection is a public good.

Economists agree that the free market will generate too little of a public good because of the free-rider problem. Each selfish citizen asks: "Why should I voluntarily pay for the good? If others finance it, they can't keep me from benefiting. But if they refuse to finance it, my contribution will be insignificant." Though not all citizens are selfish, a public good will generally be undersupplied by "the market."

It can be argued that there are at least three public goods that are relevant to the optimality of the U.S. saving rate: (1) the international ranking of the future U.S. standard of living; (2) poverty reduction for low-skilled people willing to work; (3) our contribution to the "ascent of man" through technological progress. Let me explain what each is, why each is a public good, and how this fact affects the optimality of our saving rate.

Today, the U.S. standard of living still ranks first internationally, but within a few decades our relatively low saving rate will probably move us down the ranking. If the typical American wants her grandchildren to live in a nation whose standard of living ranks first, with the psychological, political, and military corollaries of that fact, what can she do? She can of course save privately to provide for her own heirs. But she cannot influence the nation's future standard of living ranking through her own saving. That future ranking is a public good for all Americans because any selfish citizen can reason, "If others save and I don't, our future ranking will remain first, and I will enjoy that fact as much as any saver. On the other hand, if I save and others don't, my sacrifice hardly affects the future ranking."

Many citizens and politicians appear to have considerable interest in whether Japan or Germany will overtake us economically and whether our grandchildren will enjoy the most advanced economy on the globe. This implies that the international ranking of the future U.S. standard of living is a public good that many citizens value. Yet "the market" will undersupply it. It is therefore possible that many citizens would judge that they were better off if they were all induced, perhaps even compelled, to save more.

Let us now consider poverty reduction. As we explained above, most economists agree that raising the saving rate will make capital per worker rise faster, and this will make the productivity and the real wage of low-skilled workers grow faster. Hence, raising the saving rate will reduce absolute poverty faster for low-skilled people willing to work. Many citizens seem to value faster poverty reduction for such people. Yet such poverty reduction is a public good. Any selfish citizen can reason, "If others save more so that poverty declines faster, I will enjoy witnessing the reduction almost as much as any saver." So each waits for others to save for this noble purpose.

Finally, we turn to the "ascent of man." Many citizens appear to feel a pride in the quest of mankind to improve its lot and surmount new challenges. Technological progress has been a key ingredient in this historical drama. For millennia, humans have devised new products and new processes. Inventions, innovations, and breakthroughs have lifted mankind in each era. Obviously, there are dangers as well as great benefits, dislocations as well as advances. But most citizens appear willing to keep technological progress driving forward while at the same time trying to safeguard against potential hazards.

It is likely that raising the saving rate will speed the rate of technical advance and, one hopes, the ascent of man. Surely many citizens want their own generation to contribute to the ascent through further technological progress. Yet such a contribution is a public good. A selfish citizen can think, "If others save more, then technical progress will be faster and I will enjoy watching mankind's progress almost as much as any saver."

Let me summarize. A traditional economic argument for raising the saving rate contends that the current saving rate is less than the market would generate if there were no government interventions like capital income taxes, government social insurance programs, and political incentives for government dissaving. A novel economic argument for raising the saving rate is that there are at least three public goods—the international ranking of the future U.S. standard of living, poverty reduction, and the ascent of man—that are undersupplied by "the market," and that more saving is required to supply the optimal quantities of these public goods. Together, both economic arguments provide and build a strong case for policies aimed at raising the U.S. saving rate.

TECHNICAL APPENDIX

The Economy's Long-run Response to an Increase in the Saving Rate

Suppose we permanently raise our national saving rate. For example, suppose our saving rate is initially 20 percent (roughly the actual gross national saving rate of the U.S. economy), and we raise it to 24 percent permanently. How does the economy respond over the long run?

To answer this question, economists construct a growth model. A growth model can be very complicated or relatively simple. Let's consider the answer when a relatively simple model is used. The model makes several simplifying assumptions. Initially, it assumes a fixed labor force and no technological change. Capital depreciates, so new investment is required to maintain the capital stock. In the initial steady state, the 20 percent saving rate (80 percent consumption rate) provides just enough new capital to replace the capital that depreciates. To keep the numbers simple, we assume that in year 0 output per worker is 100 and consumption per worker is 80.0, as shown in Table 2.3.

Now, what happens if the saving rate is raised gradually over a half decade from 20 percent to 24 percent—a 20 percent increase—and then fixed permanently at 24 percent? The answer is shown in Table 2.3. In year 1 output per worker remains 100; the saving rate is raised to 21 percent, so the consumption rate falls to 79 percent, and consumption per worker falls to 79.0.

Since a 20 percent saving (investment) rate would have caused new capital to equal depreciation, a 21 percent investment rate causes a small rise in capital per worker and hence in output per worker in year 2. Suppose in year 2 output per worker is 101; the saving rate is raised to 22 percent, so the consumption rate falls to 78 percent, and consumption per worker is 78.8 (0.78 × 101).

Table 2.3

Response of the Economy to an Increase in Saving Rate

	Output/ worker	Consumption rate (%)	Consumption/ worker
Year 0	100	80	80.0
Year 1	100	79	79.0
Year 2	101	78	78.8
Year 3	102	77	78.5
Year 4	103	76	78.3
Year 5	104	76	79.0
Year 6	105	76	79.8
Year 7	106	76	80.6
Long run	111	76	84.4

The 22 percent investment rate again causes new capital to exceed depreciation, and results in another small rise in capital per worker and hence output per worker in year 3. As shown in Table 2.3, beginning in year 4 the consumption rate is fixed at 76 percent, and in year 7 consumption per worker is once again above its year 0 value (80.6 vs. 80.0). Eventually, even with the fixed 24 percent investment rate, diminishing returns cause new investment to no longer exceed depreciation. From then on, capital per worker stays fixed (at a level higher than its initial value), output per worker stays fixed at 111 (11 percent above its initial value of 100), and consumption per worker stays fixed at 84.4 (0.76 × 111), which is nearly 6 percent above its year 0 value of 80.0. Thus, in this example, society sacrifices for six years (consumption per worker is below its year 0 value of 80.0) and then is better off beginning in year 7. Eventually, each year consumption per worker is nearly 6 percent higher with the 24 percent saving rate than it would have been with the 20 percent saving rate.

Are we sure that in our actual economy consumption per worker will eventually exceed its initial value? Economists can show that as long as the saving rate is less than the capital (property) share of national income (roughly 30 percent in the United States; labor's share is roughly 70 percent), then consumption per worker will surpass its initial level. In fact, a saving rate equal to capital's share of national income achieves the highest possible consumption per worker in the long run. Thus, it appears safe to conclude that for increases in the saving rate that our economy might actually undertake, it is virtually certain that in the long run consumption per worker will end up higher than its initial value.

Table 2.3 assumes no labor force growth or technological progress, so if the saving rate had remained fixed at 20 percent, output would have remained fixed; consequently, when the saving rate is raised, consumption literally declines through year 4 before rising. But in a more realistic model with labor force growth and technological change, the level of consumption does not literally decline (contrary to Table 2.3) as we gradually raise our saving rate from 20 percent to 24 percent. Suppose labor force growth is 0.5 percent per year and technological change is 2.0 percent per year. Then output, consumption, and investment all normally grow about 2.5 percent per year. Envision a half-decade transition. During the half decade, our aim is to keep output growing about 2.5 percent per year while gradually raising the share of output that consists of investment goods (from 20 percent to 24 percent), while gradually reducing the share that consists of consumer goods (from 80 percent to 76 percent). This will happen if consumer goods production grows about 1.5 percent per year while investment goods production grows a little over 6 percent per year.

Here's the arithmetic. Suppose that in year 0 output is 100, consumption 80, and investment 20. If consumption grows 1.5 percent per year for five years, in year 5 it will be $80 \times (1.015)^5 = 86$. If investment grows 6.2 percent per year for five years, in year 5 it will be $20 \times (1.062)^5 = 27$. So output in year 5 will be $86 + 27 = 113$; hence output will have grown approximately 2.5 percent per year, because $100 \times (1.025)^5 = 113$. But now consumption will be 76 percent of output ($86/113 = 0.76$) and investment will be 24 percent of output ($27/113 = 0.24$). From then on, we envision the shares (76 percent, 24 percent) remaining constant so that output, consumption, and investment all grow at the same rate—a bit higher than 2.5 percent per year for many years due to the greater investment rate (24 percent vs. 20 percent). Thus, in a more realistic model with labor force growth and technological progress, during the transition to a permanently higher saving rate, consumption might grow 1.5 percent per year instead of its normal 2.5 percent per year. This below-normal growth still implies a sacrifice, but consumption does not literally decline.

The Open Economy's Long-run Response to an Increase in the Saving Rate

Thus far we have assumed a *closed* economy. But what happens if the economy is "open" to foreign borrowing or lending, to exports and imports?

To answer this question, economists have constructed a model. In order to isolate the impact of a difference in the saving rate, the model assumes that our economy and the economy of the rest of the world are identical except that saving rates differ. There's no point keeping you in suspense. Here's what the model tells us. If our saving rate exceeds the rest of the world's, then we will eventually achieve higher wealth, income, and consumption per person than the rest of the world. We will be a creditor nation and receive net interest payments from the rest of the world. We will consume more by being a net importer of goods, running a trade (in goods) deficit. But our current account will be in surplus, because our net interest earnings will exceed our trade deficit.

Conversely, if our saving rate is less than the rest of the world's, then we will eventually suffer lower wealth, income, and consumption per person than the rest of the world. We will be a debtor nation and make net interest payments to the rest of the world. We will consume less by being a net exporter of goods, running a trade (in goods) surplus. But our current account will be in deficit, because our net interest payments will exceed our trade surplus. So according to economic analysis, our *relative* saving rate—how our saving rate compares with that of the rest of the world—is one key determinant of our current account and trade balances. And our major conclusion remains unchanged in an open economy with trade and capital flows: A permanent increase in our saving rate will eventually achieve higher consumption per person.

But does the economist's model capture all the complexity of the world economy? Of course not. Is the relative saving rate really the only determinant of a nation's relative standard of living and its current account and trade balances? Of course not. Don't things like natural resource endowments, real investment opportunities, and entrepreneurship matter? Certainly they do. And aren't private property rights and free markets important? Yes, they are. Welcome to the real world. It's complicated.

But in a complicated world, we've got to simplify to make any progress. Not only that, we've got to concentrate on issues we can do something about. We can't change our basic natural resource endowment. But we can do something about our national saving rate. So that's where we focus our model and our attention. And a simple message emerges: In an open economy, as well as a closed economy, a high relative saving rate is a key factor in obtaining a high relative standard of living.

In a world of international competition, saving is a key factor. We should concentrate on achieving a high relative saving rate, thereby eventually accumulating more wealth per person than other nations. Which nation will emerge with a standard of living that is second to none? Almost surely it will be the nation that sustains the highest saving rate decade after decade.

I'm sure you want to know some of the assumptions behind our model. Let me begin by telling you its simplifications. The model has two "countries"—our country and the rest of the world (all other countries consolidated). Our country is small relative to the rest of the world, so that its behavior has little impact on the values of the rest of the world's economic variables. Except for scale, our country's economy and the world's economy are identical in every respect you can think of: they have the same population growth rate, the same production technology, and so on. And initially they have the same saving rate.

Now comes a key simplifying assumption: perfect capital mobility. This means that if savers discover they can earn a higher interest rate by lending abroad rather than at home, they shift their funds. This implies that capital will flow until the interest rate on domestic investment equals the interest rate on world investment.

But since the interest rate depends on the physical productivity of capital, and this in turn depends on capital per worker, it follows that our country and the rest of the world will always have the same capital per worker and hence the same domestic output per worker. If our capital per worker stays the same as the rest of the world's as both labor forces grow, then our domestic physical investment per worker must be the same as the rest of the world's.

I'm sure you won't be surprised to learn that with everything identical, including the saving rate, these assumptions imply that our current account and trade balances are both zero, and that the United States is neither a creditor nor a debtor nation. It turns out that our domestic absorption—consumption plus investment— exactly equals our domestic output, so that any imports are exactly matched by exports, and our trade balance is zero.

Also, our country's domestic investment exactly matches our own saving, so any interest payments our savers earn from abroad are matched by interest payments from our firms to the world's savers; thus, *net* interest payments are zero. So our current account balance, which includes payments for goods and interest, is also zero. Our wealth is equal to our domestic capital stock. We own the same amount of the rest of the world's capital stock as the rest of the world owns of our capital stock. So we are neither a creditor nor debtor nation.

But now suppose our country permanently raises its saving rate, so that our saving rate exceeds the rest of the world's. What happens? The moment our saving rate rises, our consumption rate falls. So our domestic absorption—consumption plus investment—will immediately fall below our domestic output. Thus, the excess of output over absorption will be exported, and the immediate result will be a trade surplus. With net interest payments still zero, the result will also be a current account surplus equal to the trade surplus.

But net interest payments will not remain zero. Our saving now exceeds our domestic investment. Rather than confront diminishing returns at home, our excess saving will flow abroad to finance real investment in the world economy. But this means that our savers will earn net interest payments from abroad.

As our savers accumulate wealth—claims on the world capital stock—wealth per worker and income (including interest income) per worker will rise. But this means that consumption per worker will also rise, after its initial setback. It turns out that as long as the interest rate exceeds the growth rate of labor, consumption per worker will eventually surpass its initial level. When this happens, domestic absorption (consumption plus investment) will exceed domestic output, and the trade balance will reverse. We will become a net importer of goods.

In the final steady state, we will have a current account surplus, but a trade (in goods) deficit. The net interest payments our savers earn from the rest of the world will exceed the net payments we make to buy goods. We will also be a creditor nation, owning more of the rest of the world's capital stock than it owns of our capital stock.

Note that in the short run, after we raise our saving rate, we initially run a trade (in goods) surplus. The surplus gradually becomes a deficit only after we accumulate wealth, become a creditor nation, and earn enough interest from abroad to finance higher consumption per worker than the rest of the world.

3 A PERSONAL CONSUMPTION TAX

How can we raise our saving rate? By transforming our tax system. We can state our prescription simply: Make saving tax deductible by converting the income tax to a personal consumption tax.

Many people are gripped by a fear of heresy when they hear this proposal, as if on the sixth day God had said, "Let there be an income tax." True, the income tax has been the centerpiece of the U.S. tax structure for several decades, and the propriety and wisdom of taxing income have come to be taken for granted.

Yet many economists have long advocated taxing consumption, not income. Until recently, however, it has been widely assumed—even by some of these very economists—that taxing each household's consumption might be impractical. And if economists admit that something might be impractical, you can imagine what it's like.

In the last two decades, however, a number of practical tax experts—accountants and lawyers—have concluded that a personal (household) consumption tax would be just as impractical and complicated as our income tax, but no worse. Two major studies undertaken by tax specialists—the U.S. Treasury's *Blueprints for Basic Tax Reform* (1977) and the U.K. Institute for

Fiscal Studies' *The Structure and Reform of Direct Taxation* (1978)—even concluded that replacing the income tax with a personal consumption tax would be both feasible and desirable.

Finally, in 1995, Senators Pete Domenici (Republican, New Mexico), Sam Nunn (Democrat, Georgia), and Bob Kerrey (Democrat, Nebraska) introduced a bill that would establish the Unlimited Savings Allowance Tax (USA Tax). The USA Tax would convert the personal income tax to a personal consumption tax by making all saving tax deductible. In my opinion, the definitive analysis is given by Laurence Seidman in *The USA Tax: A Progressive Consumption Tax* (1997).

The crucial difference between a personal consumption tax and an income tax is simply this: Under a consumption tax, saving would be *tax deductible;* every hundred dollars saved would be a hundred dollars that is exempt from tax. .

Does a Personal Consumption Tax Favor the Affluent?

The most common reaction to the proposal is, "It favors the affluent, who can most afford to save." But that reaction is based on a fundamental misunderstanding. Why?

The source of the reaction is the mistaken assumption that the tax rates in the tax tables will be unchanged when saving is made tax deductible. If these tax rates were unchanged, then deductibility would indeed favor the affluent, who can most afford to save.

But who says the tax rates must stay the same? In fact, if the rates were unchanged, then less total revenue would be collected due to the saving deduction, and our budget deficit would get even larger. So when we convert to a personal consumption tax and make saving tax deductible, the rates in the tax table must be raised to keep tax revenue constant. Please note that these rate increases would not raise the dollar tax payment of the average household. They would simply keep the average dollar tax payment the same despite the new saving deduction.

But how should the rate increases be apportioned among income classes? Suppose Congress wants each income class to pay the same revenue it paid under the income tax. Since high-income households save most, their tax rate must be raised most. And since low-income households save least, their tax rate must be raised least.

So we are advocating conversion of the income tax to an *equally progressive* consumption tax. How do we achieve it? Divide the population into income classes. Calculate the total tax revenue paid by each class under the current income tax. Then set the new tax rates under the consumption tax so that each income class pays roughly the same total tax as before.

Citizens disagree about how the nation's tax burden should be distributed across income classes; they disagree about how *progressive* the tax system should be. The crucial point to grasp is that making saving tax deductible by converting from an income to a personal consumption tax is neutral with respect to distribution. How the rates are set, under either an income or a consumption tax, determines how the burden is distributed across classes. The choice of tax base—income vs. consumption—is completely separate from the choice of distribution—how to set tax rates for each class. Thus, conversion to a personal consumption tax has been advocated by economists who disagree about distribution but agree about the need to raise our national saving rate. So if someone is either for or against conversion because he thinks it favors the affluent, then his reaction is based on a misunderstanding. Congress can make the new consumption tax have more, less, or the same progressivity as the current income tax, simply by adjusting the tax rates in the tax table.

The IRA Principle

Making saving tax deductible may sound like a radical departure. It isn't. We've already taken several initial steps in that direction under our income tax.

In the early 1980s, the tax law was amended to allow Individual Retirement Account (IRA) saving to be tax deductible. Unfortunately, the IRA has two key restrictions. First, there is a ceiling on the amount of annual saving that is tax deductible. Second, there is a penalty for withdrawal before retirement. As its name suggests, the purpose of the IRA is to encourage a limited amount of saving for retirement.

Under a personal consumption tax, all saving for any purpose would be tax deductible. There would be no limit on the tax-deductible amount. When funds are withdrawn to finance consumption, the consumption would be taxed. But there would be no penalty for withdrawal per se.

The IRA is not the only step we've taken toward a personal consumption tax. Under current tax law, if a person's employer contributes $1,000 to his pension fund, the employee does not pay tax on this $1,000 of income. Because $1,000 of his income has been channeled into saving, it is tax deductible for the employee. Once again, there is an important restriction: The saving must be for retirement.

These restrictions make sense if the aim is to encourage only provision for retirement. But if the aim is to keep our future standard of living second to none, then all saving warrants encouragement. To promote this objective, we must implement the IRA principle more thoroughly by making all saving tax deductible, thereby converting our income tax to a personal consumption tax.

Practical Features of a Personal Consumption Tax

But isn't it impractical to ask everyone to keep receipts of everything they buy? Even an economist can see that. The breakthrough came when some practical person realized that we don't need to add a huge number of purchase receipts to figure out a household's consumption. This ingenious person realized that all we have to do is "follow the cash." We can determine a household's consumption by adding and subtracting only a few items.

The basic insight couldn't be simpler. Almost all consumption is financed by money or checks, which I will call "cash" (perhaps with a delay made possible by a credit card). We simply follow the cash. Add the cash inflows. Subtract the non-consumption cash outflows. The remainder must have been used for consumption, so tax it. A personal consumption tax return is illustrated in the appendix to this chapter. Each line of the return is explained in Laurence Seidman's *The USA Tax: A Progressive Consumption Tax* (1997).

Here's a simplified example. Suppose a household earns $60,000 in salaries, receives $4,000 in interest and dividends, and sells stocks and bonds for $6,000, for a total cash inflow of $70,000. If the household increases its saving account balance by $8,000, and buys new stocks and bonds for $12,000, its total non-consumption cash outflow is $20,000. Therefore, its consumption is $50,000 ($70,000 minus $20,000).

I know what you're thinking. What about the treatment of housing and other consumer durables? What about the treatment of gifts and bequests? What about the borderline between consumption and saving? I won't kid you. A consumption tax has some practical problems. They have been examined in detail by experts in the *Blueprints* and elsewhere. Remember, I didn't claim that a consumption tax would be simpler than an income tax, just that it wouldn't be more complicated. I don't advocate a consumption tax for simplicity, but to protect the future standard of living. Here are some possible solutions to these practical problems.

Economists agree that when you purchase a consumer durable, like a car or a house, you are making an investment. Then you consume the services of the durable over many years. So one option is this: If you borrow to finance the durable, the loan can be excluded from cash inflow, so only the down payment is taxed in the year of purchase. But in each subsequent year, you will not be allowed to deduct the loan repayment. Thus, you will be taxed each year on the loan repayment, which is a rough approximation of your consumption that year.

When a donor gives a gift or bequest, she may get pleasure out of it. For that matter, a saver may get pleasure out of saving. But like the saver, the donor is not consuming; she is not drawing resources—land, labor, and capital—away from real investment. Her abstaining from consumption helps our future standard of living. If you favor a consumption tax to raise the future standard of living, then you should agree that the gift or bequest should be treated as tax deductible to the donor.

What about the donee—the recipient? The gift or bequest is a cash inflow. If he saves it, then he obtains an equal deduction, so the gift or bequest is not taxed. If he ever consumes it, he will be taxed in that year. If he never consumes it, then it will never be taxed. This makes sense, because as long as he abstains from consumption, he helps advance the future standard of living.

Now, some favor a consumption/gift/bequest (CGB) tax because they want the donor to be taxed. They object that under a consumption tax, gift givers will permanently escape tax, and that this is unfair. They object that donees will escape tax until they actually consume, and that this is unfair. Why is it unfair? Because, they argue, donors and donees may get pleasure or security from gifts and bequests.

But I have a different perspective. My top priority is the future standard of living. I want to reward our citizens when they help raise it. As long as they do not consume, the donor and donee are helping by releasing resources for investment. So they should not be taxed.

Incidentally, for the same reason, it makes sense to abolish all estate and gift taxes and make up the lost revenue by raising high-bracket consumption tax rates. The affluent who transfer wealth, rather than consume it, are releasing resources for investment. Abolition of estate and gift taxes, together with conversion to a personal consumption tax, gives the affluent an incentive to preserve wealth and refrain from consumption, exactly what's needed to raise everyone's future standard of living.

Finally, what about the border between consumption and investment? Let me examine one item: education. I know this will sound self-serving, coming from a professor. But the fact is that for at least two hundred years, economists have emphasized that education is an investment in human capital. Like machinery, education raises the productivity of workers. Sure, college can be enjoyable—it is partly consumption. But the investment component of a household's expenditure for education or training should be treated as tax-deductible investment under a consumption tax. Perhaps a simple rule of permitting 50 percent deductibility, up to some ceiling, would be a reasonable treatment.

Consider what this means: When you set money aside for college tuition while your child is in diapers, it is, of course, tax-deductible saving. But even when you withdraw the funds to pay tuition, half (up to a ceiling) would remain tax deductible, because an expenditure on education is partly investment.

Despite these possible solutions, there is no denying that the consumption tax has some thorny practical problems. On the other hand, a consumption tax is simpler than an income tax in certain respects. Employee compensation is complex under the income tax: should stock options be taxed as ordinary income or be given special capital gains treatment? But compensation is simple under the consumption tax: only cash received by the household is counted in its cash inflows. A capital gain is complex under the income tax: Should an attempt be made to make up for the advantage of deferring tax until the year of sale? But a capital gain is simple under the consumption tax: Only cash from the sale of stock is counted in its cash inflows. Finally, saving is complex under the income tax: Which savings vehicles (IRA, 401(k) plan) should be granted a tax deduction? But saving is simple under the consumption tax: All saving is tax deductible.

Although our focus is on the household tax, a brief comment about the business tax is warranted. A corporate income tax does not fit with a personal consumption tax. The USA Tax proposes replacing the corporate income tax with a subtraction value-added tax (VAT). Under a VAT, a business is taxed on its sales revenue minus its purchases from other firms. A VAT is a consumption tax because each business can subtract the purchase of capital goods—investment—in the year it occurs, so that firms are taxed on output (value added) minus investment, which equals consumption. Thus, the VAT makes investment tax deductible just as the personal consumption tax makes saving tax deductible. The two taxes fit together: They encourage saving and investment.

The Horizontal Redistribution Effect

Conversion to an equally progressive consumption tax will raise national saving. To help make the point as clearly as possible, two affluent persons, each with $500,000 of income, have agreed to be extremists. Person S has agreed to save everything and consume nothing, while person C has agreed to consume everything and save nothing.

Of course, emaciated S can only keep this up long enough for readers to grasp the pedagogical point. Rather than ridicule S and C for extremism, be grateful for their voluntary service in the cause of clarity. To compensate them for their service, let's flatter their egos by letting them be the only two people in the affluent $500,000 income class.

Under an income tax of 20 percent, S and C each pay $100,000 in tax, so total tax revenue is $200,000. Person S saves $400,000 and C nothing, so total saving is $400,000. Person C consumes $400,000 and S nothing, so total consumption is $400,000.

Now Congress makes saving tax deductible and converts the income tax to a personal consumption tax. What rate must Congress set for the affluent class in order to raise the same total tax revenue, $200,000? Because S and C have graciously agreed to be extremists, the answer is easy. Congressional eyes gaze insidiously on C, who alone will now pay tax. Emaciated S, though weak from lack of nourishment, manages a proud sneer, whispering that she is now exempt from tax. Since C must pay $200,000 in tax, a 40 percent consumption tax rate will do the trick because C takes no saving deduction from her cash inflow of $500,000.

What is the impact of tax conversion? Total tax revenue collected from the affluent remains $200,000. But now, instead of

$100,000 coming from each, all $200,000 comes from C. Person S, believe it or not, now saves all $500,000 of her income, instead of "only" $400,000, so total saving rises by $100,000, to $500,000. And since C is forced to cut her consumption due to her higher tax, total consumption falls by $100,000 to $300,000.

What has really happened is this: Tax conversion has caused $100,000 of cash to be redistributed from C to S, because C's cash falls by $100,000 (from $400,000 to $300,000) and S's rises by $100,000 (from $400,000 to $500,000). Person C would have consumed the $100,000, but person S saves it. Hence, total consumption falls $100,000, and total saving rises $100,000.

I call this increase in total saving due to the shifting of cash among the affluent *the horizontal redistribution effect*. It is "horizontal" because it is a shift among the affluent, not across different income classes.

Note that the horizontal redistribution effect has nothing to do with the incentive to save. Our two gracious volunteers have agreed to be impervious to incentives. They doggedly stick to their extremist behavior even when saving is made tax deductible. Person C continues to save nothing, despite the deductibility of saving. And emaciated S would no doubt save more if she could, but she can't, because she's already saving her entire income.

Through the horizontal redistribution effect, making saving tax deductible will raise total saving, even if no one responds to the greater incentive to save. This fundamental point is overlooked in the public debate, even by some sophisticated analysts. The debate over making saving tax deductible usually runs as follows. Advocates claim that the average individual will raise his propensity to save—the fraction of his after-tax income that he saves—if saving is deductible. Opponents deny it. Both sides assume that total saving will rise only if the typical individual raises his propensity to save.

But our example shows that this is not so. Extremists S and C did not change their propensity to save: S kept it at 100 percent, and C kept it at 0 percent. Each was completely unresponsive to the new incentive to save. But total saving rose through the horizontal redistribution effect. Why? Because deductibility shifted cash away from C, who would have consumed it, to S, who saved it.

The horizontal redistribution effect, of course, applies not only to the affluent, but to every income class. Congress can adjust the tax rate of each income class so that the consumption tax raises roughly the same total revenue from that class as did the income tax. But within each class, there will be a horizontal redistribution effect. Above-average savers will enjoy a tax cut, and below-average savers will suffer a tax increase. Cash will shift horizontally from persons with a relatively low propensity to save to persons with a relatively high propensity to save. So total saving will increase.

Although the horizontal redistribution effect applies to all classes, its impact is most important among the affluent. Not surprisingly, there is much more variation in the propensity to save among the affluent than among low-income households. Most low-income households save very little. But among the affluent, some households save a large fraction of their income, and others dissave—consuming more than their income. For example, in a study done by researchers at the Federal Reserve, roughly 20 percent of affluent households saved two-thirds of their income, another 20 percent saved roughly half, but 20 percent dissaved (consumed more than their income). My colleague Ken Lewis and I used the Federal Reserve data to estimate how much the horizontal redistribution effect would raise total household saving. We estimated an increase of roughly 10 percent.

We can now see whose taxes rise and whose fall by making saving tax deductible and adjusting tax rates to keep the new consumption tax as progressive as the income tax it replaces. Deductibility does not favor one income class over another. Instead, within each income class, above-average savers enjoy a tax cut and below-average savers suffer a tax increase; the average saver in the income class pays the same tax.

The Incentive Effect

Extremist C continued to consume all her after-tax income, despite the deductibility of saving. Her consumption fell only because she had less cash. But wouldn't you take advantage of the new deduction by saving a little more? Wouldn't you respond to the new incentive to save? Wouldn't the average person?

How would citizens react to the headline "Saving Now Tax Deductible"? Word would spread among ordinary taxpayers, not merely shrewd tax planners, that every hundred dollars saved is a hundred dollars not taxed. Many citizens ask: "How can I reduce my taxes?" Now there would be a clear answer: "Save." The subheadline would read: "No Restrictions." The saving can be for any purpose. It can be withdrawn without special penalty. And there is no limit to how much saving is deductible.

Note the difference between open-ended, unrestricted deductibility and IRAs. With IRAs, a person must worry about whether he is over-saving for retirement. "Suppose I need cash in five years? I'll regret that it's tied up in my IRA." But with unrestricted deductibility, the person must think no further than this year. "If I can get through this year, let me save. I can always withdraw it next year, or in five years, for any purpose, without penalty." Soon, however, a citizen will overcome his enthusiasm with this year's tax saving and face what happens in the future when he withdraws funds to finance consumption. How will the typical citizen react when he hears the IRS say: "We may not get you now, but we'll get you later"?

Some citizens may succumb in despair. "Why save when it only postpones the ax?" some will ask. But others will react: "Postponement is still worth it. After all, if I'm lucky, the world may end in the meantime." Others, however, will raise this question: "What if I cross the finish line of life never having withdrawn my savings for consumption? What if I leave a large bequest to my heirs at death?"

Good question. Some tax analysts want a bequest at death to

be taxed. They worry about letting misers sneak across the finish line of life without paying their fair share. They advocate a consumption/gift/bequest (CGB) tax instead of a consumption tax. But I'm less worried about thrifty people than I am about our nation's future standard of living. The fact is that only actual consumption, not bequests, draws resources away from investment and reduces our future standard of living. So I side with other consumption tax advocates who say: "If you cross the finish line without consuming, you win; a bequest is not consumption."

While it's only a guess, I suspect that taxing only actual consumption, not bequests, will raise our national saving rate. I have a hunch that the thought of permanently beating the IRS would inspire quite a few citizens to save more. When these citizens hear someone say, "Why save? They'll only get you later when you spend it," these citizens will reply with joy, "They'll never get me, because I'll never spend it; I'll wave it at the IRS from my deathbed and pass it on to my children and grandchildren."

The Postponement Effect

When taxes are compared, attention focuses on incentives. But there is another crucial aspect of taxes that is usually overlooked: Which tax most postpones collection over an individual's "life cycle"?

Perhaps the most important property of the consumption tax is this: it is "the great postponer." For this reason, perhaps more than any other, a consumption tax should result in a greater accumulation of capital in the economy than an income tax.

Imagine that each individual is a "life cycler." A life cycler plans ahead. He recognizes that someday he will retire, and upon retirement, alas, his income will fall further than his desired consumption. While he works, he must save, so that he can dissave in retirement to finance his consumption. Of course, not everyone is a life cycler, but enough people plan ahead, however imperfectly, to make the life cycler worth studying.

A life cycler's consumption is less than his income during

most of his work life, and greater than his income during retirement. Thus, when the income tax is converted to a consumption tax, the young person just beginning his life cycle will enjoy a tax cut during his work life and will incur a tax increase in retirement. Conversion causes postponement of some of his lifetime tax.

But this means that conversion to a consumption tax increases the ability of workers to save and accumulate wealth. Tax postponement therefore results in greater accumulation of wealth by the typical life cycler and hence a greater capital stock for the economy.

Thus, a consumption tax should achieve a higher capital stock than an income tax for three reasons: the horizontal redistribution effect, the incentive effect, and the postponement effect.

Is a Consumption Tax Equivalent to a Labor Income Tax?

Instead of a saving deduction, why not enact a capital income exemption? Under this alternative tax reform, you wouldn't get a deduction when you save. But when you earn interest, dividends, or capital gains, your capital income would be exempt from tax. Like a saving deduction, a capital income exemption gives an incentive to save.

A saving deduction converts the income tax into a consumption tax. A capital income exemption converts the income tax into a labor income tax. Both conversions give an incentive to save. For this reason, some analysts have claimed that a consumption tax is really equivalent to a labor income tax.

But it isn't. And it is crucial to understand why.

While the consumption tax is "the great postponer," the labor income tax is "the great upfronter." Under a labor income tax, the government raises all tax revenue from workers and none from retirees. So a life cycler pays all his tax "up front"—during the work stage of life. Compared to a consumption tax, a labor income tax imposes a greater tax burden on the worker, thereby reducing his ability to save. Hence, a labor income tax would achieve a smaller capital stock than a consumption tax.

In fact, the labor income tax is more of an upfronter than the regular income tax, which at least postpones some tax to retirement. So it is even possible that, despite its incentive to save, a labor income tax would achieve a lower capital stock than a regular income tax. By contrast, a consumption tax gives an incentive to save, and is also a greater postponer than an income tax, so it will clearly achieve a higher capital stock for the economy. The labor income tax gives the worker an incentive to save, but reduces his ability to do so. The consumption tax gives the worker an incentive to save, and improves his ability to do so. Since the consumption tax should result in a significantly larger capital stock than the labor income tax, it makes no sense to call them equivalent.

The two taxes also differ fundamentally with respect to fairness. The best way to communicate this difference is to shine the spotlight on a notorious character: the lazy heir. For some, the only worth of this brazen individual is his pedagogical value. For others, he is a source of secret admiration. At any rate, who is he? The lazy heir inherits a large fortune, uses it to finance a high level of consumption, never works a day in his life, and dies leaving nothing to his own children, because, he says, he doesn't wish to spoil them.

Now, what tax would the lazy heir owe under a labor income tax? Zero. At the annual April 15 news conference at his plush estate, the lazy heir holds up his tax return—an empty sheet of paper. With servants surrounding him, he complains that it is most fortunate that he owes no tax, not having worked, because he needs every bit of his fortune to maintain his mansion. Needless to say, he is a favorite on the evening news.

Under a consumption tax, however, the plight of our lazy heir would be severe. His high consumption would incur a high tax. As he sells the stocks and bonds he inherited, his cash inflow would record the sale of assets. Since there is no corresponding deduction, his taxable consumption would match his asset sales.

In fact, a consumption tax would tax the lazy heir more heavily than an income tax. Under an income tax, he would be taxed on capital income. But under a consumption tax, he would be taxed on the wealth he "decumulates" each year. Suppose the lazy heir, for spite, converts his fortune to cash, and places it under his luxurious pillow so that it earns no income. He would owe no income tax. But he would still owe substantial consumption tax.

Thus, with respect to fairness, a consumption tax is surely not equivalent to a labor income tax. Just ask the lazy heir.

How to Gradually Phase in a Personal Consumption Tax

Conversion to a consumption tax must be phased in gradually for two distinct reasons: to ensure a smooth macroeconomic transition, and to avoid double taxation. Let's consider each in turn.

First, macroeconomics. Recall what we are trying to do. We want to gradually raise the percentage of our national economic pie that goes to investment. This requires that we gradually reduce the percentage that goes to consumption. But our pie per person grows in a typical year. So it is possible to gradually reduce the percentage that goes to consumption without ever reducing the absolute size of the consumption slice per person. This should be our aim: to gradually reduce the percentage without ever reducing the absolute amount per person.

We want to slow the growth of consumer goods, so that workers who quit or retire in the consumer goods sector are not replaced, and most new jobs open up in the rapidly growing investment goods sector. But we do not want to make the output of consumer goods literally decline, because this would result in involuntary layoffs and a transitional recession. No one knows how much our population would cut its consumption demand if the entire population were converted to the consumption tax in a single year. It would therefore be completely irresponsible to convert the whole population at one time.

Now let's consider the double taxation problem. Under an income tax, a person pays tax on the income he saves, but no tax on his retirement consumption. Under a consumption tax, a person pays no tax on the income he saves, but pays tax on his retirement consumption. Now consider the "lucky" person who gets caught in the transition. He has paid tax on the income he saved. And he will also pay tax on his retirement consumption. He has a complaint: "I've been double taxed."

Here's how to handle both problems. First, for macroeconomic smoothness, the population should be converted to the consumption tax in stages. Perhaps the best method would be to phase in a cross section of the population each year over a half decade. Once you convert to the consumption tax, you convert for life. Cross-section phasing has an important advantage: because a similar mix of ages and incomes converts each year, there should be minimal disruption to the sales of particular industries.

Second, to avoid double taxation, each household would compute its "deductible old wealth" on the first day of the year it converts to the consumption tax. Its deductible old wealth would consist of wealth that would not be taxed again under the income tax, but would be taxed under the consumption tax without special protection. Wealth likely to be given as a gift or bequest is already protected because the donor would not be taxed under the consumption tax. The household would be permitted to deduct a percentage of its deductible old wealth each year over half a decade.

The Personal Consumption Tax vs. Other Consumption Taxes

What are the other consumption taxes? The retail sales tax, the value added tax (VAT), and the "flat tax." Each is simpler than the personal consumption tax, and each will raise the national saving rate. So why not abolish the income tax and replace it with one of these consumption taxes?

There's one little problem with this strategy. The current income tax is progressive: Affluent households pay a higher ratio of tax to income than non-affluent households. Replacing the income tax with either a retail sales tax, a VAT, or a flat tax would significantly shift the tax burden away from the affluent to the non-affluent. For example, in 1995 the Office of Tax Analysis of the U.S. Treasury estimated that replacing the income tax with a retail sales tax or VAT would reduce the federal tax burden of the richest 5 percent by 39 percent, and of the richest 1 percent by 55 percent. Replacement by a flat tax—where households pay a flat rate of about 20 percent above a $30,000 exemption—would reduce the federal tax burden of the richest 5 percent by "only" 21 percent, and of the richest 1 percent by "only" 36 percent—thanks to the exemption.

Now, citizens can disagree about whether this shift in the tax burden from affluent to non-affluent households is desirable or undesirable, fair or unfair. But there is no disagreement about one thing: A proposal to replace the income tax by any of these other consumption taxes will provoke a politically divisive debate between the affluent and the non-affluent. The debate over how the tax burden should be distributed will dominate the main objective: raising the national saving rate.

This is why moderate Republican Domenici and moderate Democrats Nunn and Kerrey decided to support replacing the income tax by an equally progressive personal consumption tax. Their USA Tax, introduced into the U.S. Senate in 1995, sets tax rates in its tax table that achieve roughly the same distribution of the tax burden as the income tax it replaces. The USA Tax has achieved sponsorship and support from senators of both parties. Their strategy is simple: Let's first pass a fundamental tax reform that will raise the national saving rate without shifting the tax burden from affluent to non-affluent. Once we have a personal consumption tax, we are always free to debate whether to adjust the rates in the tax table, thereby shifting the distribution of the tax burden in one direction or another.

By contrast, replacing the income tax by any other consumption tax necessarily involves shifting the tax burden from the affluent to the non-affluent. Instead of focusing on raising the national saving rate, the debate will inevitably focus on the shifting of the tax burden. USA Tax supporters do not necessarily agree about the distribution of the tax burden. But they agree that the higher priority is to achieve a tax system that promotes saving as soon as possible. They agree to first replace the income tax with an equally progressive personal consumption tax, and later debate whether to shift the distribution of the tax burden by adjusting the rates in the tax table.

Fairness: The Personal Consumption Tax vs. The Personal Income Tax

Is it fairer to tax a person according to her consumption instead of her income? The income tax advocate thinks it isn't, asserting: "Income is a better measure of ability to pay, and persons should be taxed according to their ability to pay. Consider the person with high income but low consumption. She should pay a high tax, because her ability to pay is high, not a low tax simply because she chooses to save a lot and consume a little."

The consumption tax advocate replies: "It's fairer to tax a person according to what she takes out of the economic pie rather than according to what she contributes to it. When a person produces and earns income, a contribution is made to the pool of available goods and services. Production potentially adds, rather than subtracts, from others' economic well-being. But when people actually withdraw resources for their own consumption, then these resources are not available for others to consume or businesses to invest in plant, equipment, and technology, thereby raising everyone's productivity and earnings in the future."

"But what about ability to pay?" asks the income tax advocate.

"The ability-to-pay principle," replies the consumption tax advocate, "has an element of expediency: Tax a person more, simply because the person is able to pay more. But a principle of fairness ought to consider how a person's economic behavior affects others. From this perspective, it is fairer to tax a person according to what that person subtracts from, rather than adds to, the economic pie.

Consider Connie and Sally. They have the same production and income, but Connie uses her entire income to consume goods and services for her own enjoyment, while Sally saves a large share of her income and uses only a small share to withdraw consumption goods, leaving resources for others to consume and invest. Is it really fair to tax them equally? Both have the power to consume equally. But Sally leaves more for others than Connie."

"But," asks the income tax advocate, "are you saying that if Connie consumes twice as much as Sally, she must pay exactly twice as much tax?"

"Not necessarily," replies the consumption tax advocate. "For example, under the personal consumption tax, tax rates can be set so that Connie pays more than twice the tax that Sally pays. If you want to match the distribution of the tax burden of the current progressive income tax, that's the way rates should be set. How to set the rates is a separate issue. The key point is that it is fairer to base the tax on the person's consumption rather than income."

"What about the miser with high income and low consumption?" asks the income tax advocate.

"I prefer to call him a thrifty person," replies the consumption tax advocate. "He could take a lot out of the economic pie for his own satisfaction. But he doesn't. So it is fair to charge him a low tax."

"But," continues the income tax advocate, "your thrifty person may get as much pleasure from saving as others do from consuming."

"True enough," responds the consumption tax advocate. "But we should focus on the consequences, not the motives, of each person's action. You may enjoy earning and accumulating for its own sake, but this is not sufficient reason to tax you heavily. Only when you take a huge slice of the economic pie for your own enjoyment should you be heavily taxed—not because there is anything wrong with enjoying a slice, but because it leaves less for others."

Let's Use This Powerful Tool

In chapter 2 we made the case for raising our national saving rate. Our tax system is one important tool for raising our saving rate. So let's use it. The time has come to make saving tax deductible by converting our income tax to a personal consumption tax.

APPENDIX

A Personal Consumption Tax Return

Cash Inflows

1.	Wages and salaries	$60,000
2.	Interest, dividends, cash withdrawals from business	$3,000
3.	Withdrawals from savings accounts or investment funds	$2,000
4.	Sale of stocks and bonds	$2,000
5.	Loans (excluding consumer durable loans)	$2,000
6.	Cash gifts and bequests received	$1,000
7.	Pension, social security, and insurance cash benefits	$0
8.	Total (add lines 1–7)	$70,000

Non-Consumption Cash Outflows

9.	Deposits into savings accounts or investment funds	$9,000
10.	Purchase of stocks and bonds	$7,000
11.	Loan repayments (excluding consumer durable loans)	$1,000
12.	Cash charitable contributions and gifts given	$1,000
13.	Higher education tuition (investment component)	$2,000
14.	Total (add lines 9–13)	$20,000
15.	*Consumption* (subtract line 14 from line 8)	$50,000

Deductions

16.	Personal exemptions	$10,000
17.	Family allowance	$7,000
18.	Old wealth deduction	$3,000
19.	Total (add lines 16–18)	$20,000
20.	*Taxable Consumption* (subtract line 19 from line 15)	$30,000
21.	*Tax*	$10,000
22.	Payroll tax credit	$4,000
23.	*Net Tax* (subtract line 22 from line 21)	$6,000

Each line of the tax return is explained in Laurence Seidman, *The USA Tax: A Progressive Consumption Tax* (Cambridge, MA: MIT Press, 1997).

4 CHARGE POLLUTERS A PRICE

How far we've come from the early 1970s. Remember Earth Day? Remember the homage we paid to the environment? Remember our alarm about finite natural resources? Yet thus far this book is saying—or at least seems to be saying—forget all that, let's rev up the engine of economic growth and ride roughshod over the environment in a desperate attempt to avoid losing an international economic competition. Haven't we learned anything?

I hope we have learned something. Any book calling for faster economic growth has an obligation to respond to the concern about pollution and depletion. That is what this chapter is about.

A Classic Market Failure

Let me give it to you straight. As an economist, I deny there is any problem. Whatever happens under the free market is automatically best, so pollution that occurs under a free market is "optimal," to use a favorite word among economists. Not only that, but the GDP—our beloved gross domestic product—is all that really counts. Only softheaded people care about things like the environment.

Is this your view of what the typical economist thinks about environmental pollution? I'll bet it is. Now, I could succumb to a cheap temptation. I could say, "Yes, my narrow-minded colleagues think this way, but not I. I'm a more sensitive, broad-minded economist, who recognizes that the free market isn't perfect and that the GDP isn't everything." And if I did this, I might ingratiate myself, because you might think, "He's better than the typical narrow economist, who blindly worships the free market and the GDP."

I'm tempted. But I can't do it, because I cannot live such a lie. Besides, my colleagues would never let me get away with it. The simple truth is this: All economists agree, and have agreed for many years, that the free market fails when it comes to environmental pollution. I am no better than my colleagues when I acknowledge, freely and without duress, that a free market generates too much pollution.

Not only that, but I am no better than my colleagues when I acknowledge that the GDP is a very imperfect measure of economic well-being. In particular, all my colleagues agree that environmental quality and leisure are "goods" that are as valuable to people as the material goods that are counted in the GDP.

Now, don't get me wrong. I am not going to claim that economists, as a group, are especially concerned about the environment. Some are, some aren't, like most any other group of citizens. But economists agree that if people value environmental quality, then we must judge the economy's performance by its provision of environmental quality as well as material goods. You may not associate humility with the economics profession. But most economists do pay homage—perhaps too much homage—to the humble doctrine of "consumer sovereignty." This requires a word of explanation.

In standard economics, economists refuse to judge a consumer's preferences. If the typical consumer likes apples more than oranges, who are we to judge? We take consumer preferences as given, and then ask: How well does the economy satisfy these preferences?

How do economists respond when we discover that the typical

consumer likes leisure and environmental quality as well as apples, oranges, and other material goods? Naturally we think, who are we to judge? So we give the preference for environmental quality and leisure the same respect as the preference for material goods.

Then, unanimously, we give the free market a failing grade for the poor environmental quality it generates. Even the most ardent free marketeer economists give it a failing grade in this department. But then we go a step further. We locate the source of the "market failure." The problem is that no one owns the air and water. There is a failure of property rights. May I explain?

Whenever something is "free," it is used wastefully. But anything that is owned is seldom free. Of course, the owner insists on charging a price for its use, so any potential user is deterred from frivolous use. But who owns the air above city X, or the water in river Y? No one owns it, so no one charges a price for "using" it—that is, polluting it. Is it any wonder, then, that it is polluted excessively under a free market?

For virtually all economists, including me, the solution is straightforward. The government must step in and assume ownership on behalf of the public, and then do what a typical private owner of a resource does: charge a price for its use. In other words, the market fails because a key element—ownership of a valuable resource—is absent. The solution is to restore the market by restoring the missing ingredient: ownership of the resource, and a price for its use.

There are two ways in which the government can charge a price: by tax and by permit. Under the tax method, the government sets a tax per unit of pollutant X in a particular geographic region. Polluters are then free to respond; for each unit they pollute, they must pay the tax. Under the permit method, the government decides the aggregate quantity of pollutant X it is willing to tolerate in a particular geographic region. It then auctions that quantity of permits to polluters, where each permit allows the owner to emit one unit of pollutant X. Emission of a unit of the pollutant without a corresponding permit would be illegal. The permit price would be set by supply and demand.

Note the difference between the two methods. Under the tax method, the government fixes the price per unit of pollutant X, but the response of polluters determines the aggregate quantity of pollution. Under the permit method, the government fixes the aggregate quantity of pollutant X, but the bidding of polluters determines the price of a permit—hence, the price per unit of pollutant X.

Which method is better? It depends. We'll return to this question shortly. But note this: both methods raise government revenue so the government will need less revenue from other taxes to balance its budget.

Facing the Trade-off

Now imagine a violently lethal pollutant. Even the slightest bit of it would cause enormous casualties. What do economists say about that? The same thing as any other sensible citizen: Ban it. But we economists insist on viewing a ban as an extreme case of our two pricing methods. Under the tax method, the more harmful the pollutant, the higher should be the tax per unit of pollutant; in the extreme, the tax should be so high that no polluter can afford to emit even a single unit. Under the permit method, the more harmful the pollutant, the smaller should be the aggregate number of permits that are auctioned; in the extreme, the number auctioned should be zero. So economists have no problem with an extreme case. But we insist that society face up to the basic trade-off. At any moment, society has limited resources—labor, capital, land, and raw materials. If there were just two goods that could be produced, A and B, then more of A would imply less of B. The same is true if the two goods are environmental quality and material output. More of the first implies less of the second.

Suppose we want to force pollution to zero, thereby maximizing environmental quality. The less we pollute, the more material output we sacrifice. The sacrifice can take several forms. Polluters can simply cut back their products, and resources are then shifted to products people value less. Or polluters can switch to more costly production techniques that entail less pollution. The additional cost implies that more resources are absorbed and fewer are available for other material output. Polluters, or government, can clean up pollution using resources that could have been used to make material output. However pollution is reduced, the result is a reduction in the total value of material output available for consumption.

All that economists ask is that people face up to the trade-off. Consider again a violently lethal pollutant. Here's what economists would advise. Imagine allowing a single unit to be emitted. Estimate the harm done. Then estimate the additional material output that the emission would make possible. Compare the two. If you decide that the harm outweighs the benefit from the material output, then by all means ban the pollutant.

But now consider a less harmful pollutant. Suppose that emitting a single unit would not do much damage, but would allow a highly valued increase in material output. If the public decides that the harm from the extra pollution is less than the benefit from the extra output, then by all means allow this unit to be emitted. And now make the same comparison for a second unit. If the harm is still less than the benefit, then make the same comparison for a third unit.

As the amount of pollution rises, the harm from another unit of pollution is likely to rise, and the benefit from the associated output is likely to fall. So at some point, the harm from another unit will at last exceed the benefit. Clearly, pollution should be allowed up to this point, and no further. So at last we have arrived at the socially optimal amount of pollutant X. We've properly balanced the benefit from each unit of pollutant X against its harm or cost.

It's now safe to tell you something. You've just gone through an exercise in "marginal analysis"—the most fundamental technique in microeconomics. *Marginal analysis* means finding an optimum by reasoning one unit at a time. Did it seem simple, commonsensical? Don't be alarmed, but you may be an instinctive economist.

I hope you're thinking, "It sounds nice in theory, but isn't it hard to do in practice?" Absolutely. But it would be a great step forward if people realized that there is such a thing as a socially optimal amount of each pollutant, that except in an extreme case it is greater than zero, and that in theory we can locate it by marginal analysis—reasoning one unit at time.

Now to some practical problems. Air or water quality is a "public good." This means that it is impossible to improve the quality for me without also improving it for my neighbor. Yet I may care, and he may not. The same is true of national defense, another public good, but not true of a TV, which is a typical private good. I can easily get a higher-quality TV while my neighbor sticks with his little black-and-white model. But not so for environmental quality or national defense.

Imagine that the government conducts a survey. An interviewer asks each citizen: "Be honest, how much would you pay to raise air quality from grade F to grade D?" Then the government sums the amount all honest citizens would be willing to pay, and compares it to the cost—the lost material output. If the sum of payments exceeds the cost of lost output, air quality should be increased to grade D. And then the government asks the same question about raising it from grade D to grade C. Once the sum of what people are willing to pay no longer exceeds the cost of another unit of quality, the government has arrived at the socially optimal grade of quality.

But there's a little practical problem. How can the government get citizens to be honest? After all, what would you think if a government interviewer came to your door and asked, "How much are you willing to pay for Z?" You might think, "If I tell him I'd be willing to pay $100 for Z, that's actually what he'll force me to pay." I'm sure *you* would be honest, but I'll bet you know someone who would understate his true willingness to pay.

Economists have tried to invent ingenious techniques to induce citizens to answer honestly. But although some progress has been made, such techniques are not often used. So we must admit that determining the socially optimal amount of pollutant X will be as imperfect, in practice, as determining the optimal amount of national defense or police protection. Imperfectly, the legislature must simply do the best it can to weigh cost against benefit.

Why Economists Advocate Pollution Prices

What's so great about using prices for pollution? Once the target for pollutant X in a particular region is set, why not just assign a quota (ceiling) to each polluter of X, to ensure that the aggregate quantity of X equals our target?

Now we come to the heart of the matter. Once the aggregate target has been set, how do we decide which firms should do the polluting—that is, how do we "allocate" pollution among the polluters? For example, suppose our aggregate target for pollutant X in region R is 1,000 units, and there are 100 polluters of X in the region. One simple approach would be to allow each polluter to emit 10 units of X. Another approach would be for the government to mandate specific low-pollution production techniques for the polluters of X. In fact, this "technology-forcing" approach is generally taken by the U.S. government. Unfortunately, each of these approaches would be a poor way to handle the allocation problem. Why?

First of all, the 100 polluters of X produce a variety of products. Consumers value some of these products more than others. Surely we want the allocation to take account of consumer preference for the products. Second, the polluters differ in technological options. Some can cut back pollution easily with little additional cost. Others must incur a substantial cost increase to achieve the same reduction. Since polluters will pass on cost increases to consumers, we want the allocation to take account of these technological options.

It might seem that government agents could interview consumers about their preferences for products, and the polluters about their technological options. But these interviews would be costly and of dubious value. It's far from obvious what questions to ask consumers. And while the questions are clearer for the polluters, why should they tell the truth? Wouldn't any polluter try to exaggerate the cost of cutting back in order to win a higher ceiling?

I'm sure you've realized by now that interviews could also be used to decide how much to produce of any product, pollution aside. Fortunately, we don't use them. Instead, our price system gets the job done. Both consumers and producers respond to prices, and there is no need for government interviewers.

Let's see how pollution prices would handle the allocation problem. First, consider the tax method. Suppose the government sets a tax of $20 per unit of pollutant X. The polluter whose products have good substitutes will reason: "I can't afford to pay this tax on many units, because when I try to pass the cost on to my customers by raising my price, they will simply shift to substitutes." By contrast, the polluter whose products are highly valued by consumers will reason: "I can afford to pay the tax, because when I try to pass the cost on to my customers, I will succeed." So who ends up cutting pollution sharply? The polluter whose product has good substitutes. And who ends up cutting back relatively little? The polluter whose product is highly valued by consumers. And this is exactly the pattern of cutback we want.

Next, consider the polluter with technological options that enable a reduction in pollution at little additional cost. He reasons: "Rather than pay the tax, it is cheaper for me to switch technologies and reduce pollution." By contrast, consider the polluter with few technological options. Only at high cost can he reduce pollution. He reasons: "I'm still better off paying the tax, because it would be even more expensive for me to switch technologies." So who cuts back pollution sharply? The polluter with good technological options. And who cuts back pollution relatively little? The polluter with few technological options. And this is exactly the pattern of reduction we want.

Of course, when each polluter of X decides how much to pollute if the tax is $20, it may turn out that aggregate pollution of X in the region will be 1,200 or 800 instead of the target, 1,000. If pollution is 1,200, then the government should raise the tax above $20; if pollution is 800, then the government should lower the tax below $20. Eventually, the government will find the tax that approximately achieves the aggregate target of 1,000.

Now consider the permit method. The government would auction off 1,000 permits by asking polluters to place orders for permits at each of the following prices: $5, $10, $15, $20, $25, $30, $35. The polluters would submit their orders at each price. For example, at a price of $10, polluters might order 1,200, while at a price of $30, polluters might order 800. Suppose that at a price of $20, polluters would want to order 1,000. The government would then announce that the permit price is $20 and would sell each polluter the number of permits it ordered at that price.

Suppose the permit price is $20 per unit of pollution. Then a $20 per unit pollution tax should produce exactly the same pattern of pollution reduction across polluters and yield aggregate pollution equal to 1,000. After all, a polluter doesn't care whether the $20 price per unit is called a permit price or a tax. He will figure his profit and do the same thing. Therefore, whether the price is charged through the tax or permit method, the desirable pattern of cutback across polluters is induced. So we see how a price system results in the socially optimal allocation of pollutant X across polluters. Is some more general principle at work here? Of course. A price system results in the socially optimal allocation of any resource across users—whether the resource is labor, capital, materials, or pollutant. One requirement of being an economist since Adam Smith is to understand this point. And that is why economists want to use prices to allocate pollution among polluters.

There is another way to put this. We can fight over what the target for pollutant X should be. Should it be 800 units or 1,200 units instead of 1,000? I've already admitted that it is tough to answer this question in practice, and economists don't claim to offer any good way of selecting the target. But once the target has been set, we can surely agree on this: Let's achieve the pollution target with the minimum sacrifice in material output.

That is exactly what pollution prices can do. Pollution prices induce a socially desirable pattern of pollution reduction across polluters. This means that the target is achieved with the minimum loss in the value of material output.

The Passionate Objector

But alas, a passionate objector has risen to his feet and will keep silent no longer. He cries, "Isn't a pollution price a 'license to pollute' and therefore reprehensible?" I'm afraid, my passionate friend, that you've confused two distinct tasks: First, what should be the aggregate target? Second, given the target, how should we allocate the pollution among polluters? Prices apply only to the second task, while you are really concerned about the first task—the setting of the target. No doubt you want a target of zero. Fine; make your case, and we will listen. If you succeed, then we will simply ban the pollutant. But if you fail to convince us and we decide to tolerate a certain amount of pollutant X, then surely even you will agree that we should achieve the target with the minimum sacrifice in material output. And that's where prices come in.

Our passionate objector shifts his ground and asks, "Won't the polluters just pass on these pollution prices to me, an innocent consumer, by raising product prices to cover these charges?" Yes, answers any honest economist, they certainly will. "And," continues our righteous objector, "why should I pay for their foul pollution? Let them pay for it!"

I'm afraid, my passionate objector, that once again you have missed the point. The whole object of pollution prices is to confront consumers with the environmental cost of the products they buy. The price system is an information system. The price of each product is supposed to convey information to the consumer—namely, the cost of producing it. If the price is less than cost, then the consumer is misled and demands too much of the good; if the price is greater than cost, then the consumer demands too little of the good. The free market fails because the price of high-polluting (HP) output is too low relative to the price of low-polluting (LP) output. Why is the price of HP output too low? Because it does not include the environmental cost. And why not? For the simple reason that polluters are not charged for polluting. And why aren't they charged? Because there is no owner of air or water to impose the charge. So consumers are induced, by the false price signals, to consume too much HP output and too little LP output. The whole point of pollution prices is to raise the price of HP output relative to the price of LP output, so that consumers receive accurate information, and as a result shift consumption from HP to LP products.

"But is this fair?" replies our objector. "Is it fair that I, an innocent consumer, should pay, instead of the dirty polluters?"

I beg your pardon, but what do you mean, innocent? You are enjoying a product that entails pollution. Yes, the producer did the dirty work, and now you want to enjoy the product without any responsibility for what its production required. How admirable!

Also, to whom do you want to shift the burden? The inanimate corporation? Alas, there is a little obstacle to your strategy, and it is this: Business firms don't bear burdens; only people do. The people may be consumers, workers, stockholders, or managers. But it is ostrichlike to hope that lifeless corporations, not flesh-and-blood people, will bear the burden. So the debate is really about which people should bear it. Most economists take this position: Let each consumer pay a price that reflects the cost of the product, including the environmental cost, so that the price system conveys accurate information.

Somewhat subdued, our objector at last asks a better question. "But aren't there some practical problems with your two pricing methods that you've been concealing?"

Well, *concealing* isn't the right word. But I'll admit I haven't gotten around to them. So let's consider a few problems. Perhaps the most important practical problem is this: Pricing requires metering—measuring each polluter's emissions—while mandating low-pollution technologies does not. In some cases, metering may be too costly or unfeasible. Naturally, economists recommend using pricing only if the cost of metering is less than the benefit of pricing.

The tax method has another problem: It can never guarantee that the pollution target will be met precisely. In response to a given tax per unit, polluters may emit too much or too little. If too much, the government can raise the tax; if too little, the government can lower it. But the government may never hit it exactly right. Of course, we should keep this problem in perspective. Earlier, we saw that selecting the target is extremely difficult in the first place. No selected target should be regarded as sacrosanct, because it surely differs from the social optimum. So moderately missing the target should not be viewed with alarm, because the target itself is probably not the social optimum.

While the permit method seems to guarantee that the target will be achieved, it has other problems. Will the auction occur on a single day for the year? What if a firm decides it needs more or fewer permits as the year progresses? Will the permits be transferable? Will there be a continuous resale market for permits? Who will be allowed to bid for permits? Will firms buy permits simply because they expect to sell the permits at a higher price, or because they want to keep competitors from getting the permits they need to produce? The tax method has none of these problems.

Thus far, neither the United States nor any other nation has relied heavily on pollution prices to implement environmental policy. Should economists surrender to despair? Not at all. The cause of pollution prices has slowly begun to make progress. Some recent experiments with pollution prices (in the form of transferable permits) give grounds for hope. Nevertheless, we must confess that governments still generally mandate specific production techniques for polluters. So we continue to achieve a given level of environmental quality with an unnecessarily large sacrifice in material output.

Faster Growth and Pollution

Will faster growth doom us to more pollution? Not necessarily. Suppose that today, 100 units of output are accompanied by 10 units of pollution. Isn't it inevitable that 200 units of output will be accompanied by 20 units of pollution? Not necessarily. The key to breaking the link between output and pollution is substitution of less-polluting goods for more-polluting goods, and of low-pollution production technology for high-pollution production technology.

Material output consists of many goods and services. With today's technology, some are high-pollution (HP) and others are low-pollution (LP). Even if technology remained the same, we could raise our total output without raising pollution if we shifted the composition of our output from HP to LP goods.

How can we induce such a shift? I'm sure you can guess: by gradually raising our set of pollution prices as our output grows. This will raise the price of HP goods relative to the price of LP goods, and consumers will be induced to shift their demand from HP to LP goods. Producers will therefore be compelled to shift production from HP to LP goods.

Moreover, production technology can be shifted as output grows. Many goods can be produced using alternative methods that generate different amounts of pollution. We could raise our total output, without increasing pollution, by shifting from high- to low-pollution production technologies, using pollution prices as a deterrent against the use of HP technology. Such prices would make it profitable for firms to reduce the pollution that accompanies output by shifting to low-pollution production technologies.

So can we grow faster without reducing environmental quality? Yes. But to do so, we must gradually raise our set of pollution prices as our output grows, thereby inducing these substitutions as growth takes place.

It is true that as output grows, it gets "harder" to maintain a given level of environmental quality in this sense: If nothing were done to change the mix of HP and LP goods, or the mix of HP and LP production technologies, then environmental quality would deteriorate. All the more reason for using pollution prices (through taxes or auctioned permits), rather than mandated production techniques, to implement environmental policy. The more importance we attach to raising output per person, the more important it is to maintain environmental quality with the minimum sacrifice in material output.

Faster Growth and Depletion

Will faster growth be stalled by resource depletion? Again, not necessarily. Suppose that today, 100 units of output is accompanied by the depletion of 10 units of a natural resource. Isn't it inevitable that 200 units of output will be accompanied by the depletion of 20 units of the natural resource? Fortunately, not necessarily.

Would it surprise you to learn that the key to breaking the link between output and natural resources is substitution of goods whose production requires low amounts of natural resources (LR goods) for goods whose production requires high amounts of natural resources (HR goods), and of LR production technologies for HR production technologies?

Material output consists of many goods and services. With today's technology, some are "high-resource-using" (HR), and others are "low-resource-using" (LR). Even if technology stayed the same, we could raise our total output, without raising depletion, if we shifted the composition of our output from HR to LR goods.

How can such a shift be induced? I'm sure you can guess: by a rise in natural resource prices. If this happens, the price of HR goods will rise relative to the price of LR goods, consumers will be induced to shift demand from HR to LR goods, and producers will therefore be compelled to shift production from HR to LR goods.

Moreover, production technology can be shifted as output grows. Many goods can be produced with alternative technologies that utilize different amounts of natural resources. We could raise our total output, without raising depletion, by shifting from high- to low-resource-using production technologies.

How can such a shift be induced? I'm absolutely sure you can guess: by a rise in natural resource prices. If this happens, it will be profitable for firms to reduce the depletion that accompanies output by shifting to low-resource-using production technologies.

But now we come to an important difference between pollution and depletion. The government sets the pollution tax or the volume of permits for auction, so it is up to the government to raise the tax or limit the volume of permits (resulting in a higher permit price) as output grows. The government must act because of the absence of private ownership of air and water. But there is private ownership of natural resources and it is the market that sets resource prices. So the key question becomes: Will the market raise resource prices as output grows?

The best way to know the answer is to imagine, pleasantly, that you are a resource owner. Your resource lies underground, and you have the option of mining it and selling it to firms for production today, or holding it in the ground to await a future price. What do you do? How much do you mine and sell, and how much do you keep underground?

Suppose you read that scientists are on the verge of a breakthrough that will provide a cheap, abundant substitute for your resource. As a citizen, you are overjoyed at the advance of mankind through brainpower. As a resource owner, you are desperate. There is no point holding your resource underground to await a future price. So you mine and sell at full capacity.

Now suppose that instead, you read that scientists regard such a breakthrough as unlikely, so your resource, growing scarcer each year, will command a rising price in future years. As a citizen, you are in despair over the failure of brainpower to advance mankind. As a resource owner, you can hardly conceal your glee. Why sell to the market today when a much higher price awaits you in the future? Even if you need cash, it would be better to borrow than to foolishly mine and sell at full capacity. So you hold most of your resource underground, as do other owners of that resource. Its price rises immediately, inducing firms to cut down on current utilization.

But look what has happened. Lo and behold, conservation has

been achieved. You and your fellow resource owners have cut down mining and selling, and kept most of your resource underground. Of course, your motive was not exactly noble. In fact, the word *conservation,* with its public-spirited connotation, never entered your mind. In truth, the word "profit," not "conservation," was on your smiling lips as you fell asleep each night.

But old Adam Smith would not have been surprised. In your pursuit of profit, you advanced the public welfare. With the threat of your resource becoming scarce in the future, the market gave you a profit signal to conserve now. And so you did. Immediately, your cutback in mining and selling raised your resource's price and induced a cutback in its utilization. We did not have to rely on your benevolence, but only your self-interest, to slow the depletion of your resource. So without any government action, the market will automatically tend to generate the desired rise in the price of a resource as output grows if the resource is really becoming scarce.

We haven't even mentioned another important consequence of the rise in current prices and anticipated future prices: You and your fellow miners will go exploring. With high prices, more exploration is worth it. Also, scientists will go to work trying to invent substitutes. With high prices, there's a lot of money to be saved in finding alternatives. So not only do high prices cut current use, they also create incentives for long-term solutions.

Can it really be this simple? Unfortunately, no. The market can make mistakes. After all, no one has a crystal ball. Everyone may underestimate the difficulty of finding substitutes for your resource. So everyone may underestimate the future price of your resource. You and other owners may decide to mine and sell too much today. In the future, everyone may regret it.

So it would be naive to believe that the market handles the depletion problem perfectly. But it should be some consolation that the market has the tendency to conserve any resource that threatens to grow scarce in the future, and to induce the invention of substitutes.

Substituting Capital for Resources

Suppose we believe that some important resources will grow scarce in the future. Should we save more or less? Should we accumulate more capital—physical, human, and knowledge—or less? A moment's reflection should tell us that our best chance to stave off a future decline in our standard of living is to save more, accumulating more capital that can substitute for the resources being depleted.

The production of output depends on labor, capital, and natural resources. If labor grows scarce, more capital can make up for it. Similarly, if natural resources grow scarce, then once again, our best chance for preserving output is to have more capital to make up for it. Probably the most important capital to accumulate is knowledge capital: the blueprints of how to make new products, and how to make the same products differently. If we see resources vanishing, we need to cut our consumption and devote more of our labor force to investment in knowledge capital in order to invent ways around the coming depletion.

So capital accumulation and conservation are allies, not enemies. If a resource is being depleted, there are two things we can do to try to protect our future: We can conserve by cutting down on current utilization of the resource, and we can accumulate more capital—especially knowledge capital—so that we are able to get by with less of the resource in the future. Concern about resource depletion is no reason to cut saving and capital accumulation. On the contrary, it is an important reason to save more and accumulate capital faster.

Does it surprise you that conservation and capital accumulation are allies? It shouldn't. Both are ways of protecting the future standard of living, and both require sacrifices in current consumption. Those who care little about the future will deplete and consume. But those who want to protect the future will conserve and save.

5 A NORMAL UNEMPLOYMENT BALANCED BUDGET RULE (NUBAR)

Should the government try to balance its budget every year? Most citizens say yes, but most economists say no. Economists believe that it would be dangerous to try to balance the budget every year. There is, however, a safe balanced budget rule. I call it NUBAR—my own acronym—which stands for "normal unemployment balanced budget rule," and which reads as follows: "Congress shall enact a *planned* budget for the coming fiscal year that technicians *estimate* will be balanced *if next year's unemployment rate is normal (the average of the preceding decade)*."

You'll admit that NUBAR is not very complicated. But you're probably thinking, why not make it even simpler by dropping that clause about the normal unemployment rate? Unfortunately, without that little clause, the balanced budget rule would be dangerous: It would require congressional action in the middle of a recession that might turn it into a depression.

Throughout this chapter, I will assume that it is a good thing to have a properly constructed balanced budget rule for Congress. Some economists disagree, but I will leave their arguments for the appendix to this chapter. In my view, it is a good thing because legislators need fiscal discipline. They will often be tempted to propose an increase in spending, or a cut in taxes, because both actions are popular. But a balanced budget rule imposes some discipline. With a rule, legislators must face the fact that raising spending will require raising taxes, and cutting taxes will require cutting spending. They will think twice before proposing an increase in spending, because opponents will point out that their proposal requires an increase in taxes. And they will think twice before proposing a cut in taxes, because opponents will point out that their proposal requires a cut in government spending. The simplest way to impose this discipline is to enact a balanced budget rule.

An Always-balanced Budget Rule Could Turn a Recession into a Depression

To many citizens, the remedy for government deficits seems simple: Require a balanced budget every year. According to this view, the planned budget should always aim at balance, based on the best available forecast. Once the fiscal year has begun, if a deficit begins to emerge, a prompt cut in spending or increase in taxes to restore balance should be required. I'll call this an "always-balanced budget rule." Another name might be "the no ifs, ands, or buts balanced budget rule" or "the no excuses balanced budget rule." The rule is so simple. It's a shame it suffers from a fatal defect: It would destabilize the economy. Why?

Suppose the economy is operating at a normal level of output when the budget for next year is planned. Technicians advise Congress on where to set tax and spending rates so that if the economy remains at a normal unemployment rate, the budget will be balanced.

How do the technicians arrive at their conclusion? They estimate how much tax revenue will be raised—given the statutory tax rates—if the economy is normal and national income is normal; they then compare this revenue to estimated expenditure. Make note of this: If national income turns out to be below normal, then tax revenue will be lower than the technicians' estimate.

As the fiscal year begins, suppose the economy falls into recession. National income falls below normal and, automatically, tax revenue falls below the level that planners estimated. Hence, the budget moves into deficit.

If you are inclined to blame Congress for everything, please note that this particular deficit is not the fault of Congress. The source of this deficit is the unexpected recession. But this is a "no excuses" balanced budget rule. Even though Congress did not cause the deficit, it must act promptly to eliminate it. Under the always-balanced rule, Congress must promptly cut spending or raise tax rates to eliminate the deficit brought on by recession.

What happens to the economy, already in recession, when Congress cuts spending or raises taxes? Suppose Congress cuts government purchases. For example, it cuts the purchase of planes for the military, and computers for government offices. Then the producers of planes and computers suffer a fall in orders and hence cut production. Their employees earn less income and in turn cut their consumer spending. The recession deepens.

Or suppose Congress cuts cash transfers. For example, it cuts spending on welfare, food stamps, and college financial aid. Then the recipients of these transfers have less to spend, and producers observe a decline in demand. They cut production. Their employees earn less income and in turn cut their consumer spending. Once again, the recession deepens.

Finally, suppose Congress raises tax rates. Taxpayers have less after-tax income, cut their spending, and the result is the same: an intensification of the recession. Thus, no matter how Congress tries to eliminate the recession-induced deficit, it makes the recession worse. For decades, economics textbooks have emphasized that an always-balanced budget rule is destabilizing: It risks turning a recession into a depression.

Drama in the United States Senate

Unfortunately, a majority of U.S. senators were willing to take the risk in 1995 and again in 1997. In both years, after weeks of debate and intense lobbying by both sides, the Senate came within a single vote of the two-thirds majority (67 out of 100) required to pass a balanced-budget amendment to the U.S. constitution. Under this particular amendment, federal government spending cannot exceed tax revenue, even in a recession or depression, because borrowing is *prohibited*, unless there is a three-fifths vote of both houses to suspend the prohibition. In 1995, a few weeks before the Senate voted, the House had obtained the necessary two-thirds majority (290 out of 435) by passing the amendment with over 300 votes in favor. Passage by the Senate would have sent the amendment to the state legislatures for ratification; three-fourths of the legislatures would be required. In 1997, the Senate voted first, and when passage failed by one vote, the House postponed its vote.

Most advocates of the amendment conceded that it would be a mistake to balance the budget in the middle of a recession. They emphasized that their amendment contained an escape clause: if three-fifths (60 out of 100) of the Senate and the same fraction (261 out of 435) of the House of Representatives voted to suspend the prohibition in any year, then borrowing would be permitted and a deficit allowed.

I share the view of most economists: relying on a suspension is playing with fire. Here's why. Under the amendment, as soon as the economy drops unexpectedly into recession, tax revenue falls below planned spending. With borrowing prohibited until a suspension is enacted, the government must immediately cut its spending, intensifying the recession. Now, how long will it take to get the suspension enacted? First, a suspension won't be seriously considered until the evidence is clear that the economy is indeed in a recession. But it takes the government several months to collect the data to confirm a genuine recession. Second, once a recession is undeniable, a fierce debate will begin. While some legislators will advocate suspension, others will oppose it, and others will stay undecided for a long time. Why?

Senator Sincere may oppose suspension because he really believes that a suspension will make the recession worse. On the floor of the Senate, he passionately argues, "Now is the time to keep our pledge to the American people to balance the budget. To get out of this recession, we must restore business confidence and consumer confidence. Abandoning our commitment will weaken public confidence just when it needs to be restored."

Senator Opportunism may oppose suspension because he knows the public doesn't understand the purpose of the suspension, and he can gain politically by ridiculing the suspension. On the floor of the Senate, he says, "There are those who would use the excuse of the recession to break our promise to the American people. But I will stand behind our commitment in bad times as well as good."

Finally, Senator Logroller makes no speech on the Senate floor. He announces he is undecided on this difficult issue and invites his colleagues to persuade him in private discussions. In those discussions, he says, "You're here to persuade me how to vote on the suspension. I honestly cannot decide whether suspension would help or hurt the economy. But I do know that I need your vote for my own bill—a measure that will help the country and my own state. Can I count on your support for my bill?"

Not surprisingly, quite a few senators and congressmen turn out to be undecided on the suspension and eager to have private discussions with colleagues on both the suspension and their own favorite legislation.

And so, as the recession deepens, floor debate and private discussions drag on. The advocates of suspension try desperately to get three-fifths of the senators and congressmen to commit themselves to vote for suspension, but just when they think they've got the votes, several quietly let it be known that they are once again undecided and need more private discussion.

Now, does this prove that a prompt suspension cannot be enacted? No. But it certainly proves that a prompt suspension cannot be counted on. No one knows what Congress would do in a recession. But that uncertainty is enough for most economists. Why risk turning a recession into a depression?

Along with other economists, for several weeks in both 1995 and 1997 I spent a great deal of time mailing, phoning, and faxing the message, "Don't risk a depression," to staff advisers of undecided senators. Every day newspapers would report the latest head count: "Amendment supporters say they have over sixty votes and believe they will win enough of the undecideds to get the necessary sixty-seven." In both years, when the vote was finally taken, sixty-six voted in favor, and the amendment failed by one vote. It is not often that something so important is decided by a single vote.

In both years, the thirty-four senators who voted no cited objections other than the depression risk. Some wanted Social Security excluded, others wanted a separate capital budget, and still others feared that the amendment would prove unenforceable. But many of the thirty-four stated that the risk of depression was one reason they voted no.

Most advocates of the amendment conceded that there was a small risk of depression, but they asserted that it was a risk that must be taken to balance the budget. But this assertion is untrue. There is a way to write a balanced budget rule that involves no depression risk.

NUBAR

The following simple balanced budget rule would avoid the depression risk: "Congress shall enact a *planned* budget for the coming fiscal year that technicians *estimate* will be balanced *if next year's unemployment rate is normal (the average of the preceding decade).*" I call this rule NUBAR (normal unemployment balanced budget rule). The technicians should probably be the employees of the Congressional Budget Office (CBO), who already perform similar tasks for Congress.

Note two crucial features of NUBAR: First, it applies to this year's *planned* budget for next year, not this year's actual spending and revenue. Second, it is *not* based on a *forecast* of next year's economy. Technicians are instructed to estimate spending and tax revenue on the assumption that next year's unemployment rate will be normal, whether or not they forecast a normal unemployment rate for next year.

Assume the technicians are accurate in their estimates about what spending and tax revenue will be if next year's unemployment rate is normal. If next year's unemployment rate turns out to be normal, the budget will be balanced; if next year's unemployment rate turns out to be above normal (national output, income, and tax revenue below normal), the budget will run a deficit; and if next year's unemployment rate turns out to be below normal (national output, income, and tax revenue above normal), the budget will run a surplus. On average, but not in every year, the budget will be balanced. Even if the technicians make errors in particular years, as long as the errors are unbiased, on average the budget will be approximately balanced.

With NUBAR, what happens if the economy falls into recession? Automatically, tax revenue falls and a budget deficit results. Under NUBAR, Congress is not required to immediately raise taxes or cut spending in the recession because NUBAR applies to the *planned* budget, not current spending and revenue.

What about the budget that is planned in the middle of recession for the coming fiscal year? Under NUBAR, Congress must set spending and tax rates so that technicians estimate that the planned budget will be balanced *if and only if* the economy returns to a normal unemployment rate next year. Suppose someone objects, "But this year's recession is so deep that output, income, and tax revenue will still be below normal next year, so next year the actual budget will show a deficit."

A NUBAR advocate should reply, "That's exactly what we want. We don't want to achieve a balanced budget next year if the economy is still in recession. Why not? Because to achieve a balanced budget next year in recession, this year we would have to plan higher tax rates, and lower spending rates, than NUBAR requires. But these higher tax rates and lower spending rates would reduce total spending in the economy next year, making next year's recession worse. We expect NUBAR to result in an actual deficit in recession, and an actual surplus in a boom. That's what we want."

NUBAR is not a novel proposal. For many years, economists have recommended that Congress try to balance the planned budget on the assumption that next year there is *full* employment. The only difference is that NUBAR requires the technicians to assume that there will be a normal unemployment rate (the average of the preceding decade), instead of assuming that there will be full employment. Thus, the basic strategy of NUBAR has long been advocated by economists.

There are, however, two differences between NUBAR and the full employment balanced budget rule. First, NUBAR avoids a debate about what is "full employment." Instead, NUBAR uses the normal unemployment rate as its benchmark. The normal unemployment rate is defined as the average of the preceding decade. "Normal" is not necessarily "optimal" or "full."

Second, NUBAR will achieve an average budget deficit, over a decade, that is close to zero, because it is based on a realistic unemployment rate—the actual average of the preceding decade. A full employment budget rule will achieve an average budget deficit, over a decade, that is much greater than zero. The reason is that, in practice, Congress will undoubtedly define "full employment" more ambitiously than normal employment.

For example, under NUBAR, if the average unemployment over the preceding decade has been 6 percent, then NUBAR will require a planned budget that is estimated to be balanced on the assumption that the economy's unemployment rate will be 6 percent. We do not claim 6 percent is "optimal" or "full"; it is simply realistic, "normal." A full employment balanced budget rule might require a planned budget that is balanced on the assumption that the economy's unemployment rate will be, say, 5 percent, or even 4 percent. But when the economy's unemployment rate turns out, on average, to be closer to 6 percent, this planned budget will result in a deficit. Thus, in practice, NUBAR will on average balance the budget, while a full employment balanced budget rule will not.

NUBAR Is Neutral

NUBAR makes fiscal policy neutral. In sharp contrast to the always-balanced rule, NUBAR avoids destabilizing the economy. But it is true that NUBAR does not permit a shift in the planned budget that would try to combat a recession or boom.

A rule could be designed that would require shifts in the planned budget to stabilize the economy. In a recession, the rule would require higher planned spending and/or lower planned taxes than NUBAR, so the planned budget would add more total spending to the economy than the NUBAR planned budget. In a boom, the rule would require a lower planned spending and/or higher planned taxes than NUBAR, so the planned budget would add less total spending to the economy than the NUBAR planned budget. Such a rule would probably be better than NUBAR. But it would also be more complex and more difficult for legislators and citizens to understand. If economists press for this rule, it is likely that Congress will reject it as too complex and unintelligible, and we will continue to have no rule. A better strategy is to urge Congress to adopt NUBAR. Once a NUBAR statute is enacted, we can then consider whether NUBAR should in turn be replaced by the more complex stabilizing rule.

But if NUBAR is neutral, who will stabilize the economy? The answer, we will argue in chapter 6, is our central bank, the Federal Reserve. The Federal Reserve is the institution best suited to bear the responsibility for stabilizing the economy by the proper conduct of monetary policy.

In contrast to Congress, which has hundreds of tasks, the Fed has only a few. It meets monthly, relatively insulated from political pressure, to adjust monetary policy with the aim of stabilizing the economy. It has a talented staff of well-trained economists who focus on this task. If the economy is in recession, the Fed raises the money supply, reducing interest rates to provide stimulus. If the economy is in a boom, the Fed contracts the money supply, raising interest rates to provide restraint.

NUBAR would make the Fed's task easier. The Fed cannot set the proper monetary policy unless fiscal policy is predictable. With no rule governing fiscal policy, the Fed must guess what Congress will do. This is no easy task. But if Congress is constrained by NUBAR, the Fed can plan more effectively.

The burden of stabilizing the economy should not be assigned to Congress. Instead, the aim should be to constrain Congress so that, on average, the budget is close to balance and destabilizing budget shifts are avoided. Given this neutral, predictable fiscal policy, it should then be the Fed's job to stabilize the economy.

Of course, in the unlikely event of a very severe recession, NUBAR should be suspended so that fiscal policy can join monetary policy in preventing a depression. In such an economic emergency, Congress should be free to cut taxes and raise spending by more than NUBAR would allow in order to help raise total spending in the economy until recovery is solidly under way.

Should NUBAR Be a Statute or a Constitutional Amendment?

Table 5.1 shows that, without either a statute or a constitutional amendment, progress has been made in the 1990s in moving the federal budget toward balance and halting the rise in the ratio of federal debt to GDP. As of the mid-1990s, the federal deficit and federal debt as a percentage of GDP were low compared to other economically advanced countries. There is no emergency.

However, there are storm clouds on the distant horizon. Social Security surpluses are included in the budget figures in the table; without them, the deficit would be roughly 1.0 percent greater (for example, in 1996 the deficit excluding Social Security would be about 2.4 percent instead of 1.4 percent). Social Security surpluses are projected to become deficits in about two decades. As the baby boomers begin retiring and longevity continues to increase, Medicare is projected to grow at a rapid rate. So pressures will build on the government budget. It therefore seems prudent to enact a NUBAR statute now and redesign the constitutional amendment to embody NUBAR instead of the dangerous always-balanced budget rule. As pressure builds, we can observe whether the NUBAR statute is strong enough to handle it. If not, the time may come to give a NUBAR constitutional amendment serious consideration.

Table 5.1

Federal Budget Data, As a Percent of Gross Domestic Product, GDP

Year	Receipts	Outlays	Surplus or deficit	Debt held by public
1960	17.8	17.8	+0.1	45.7
1961	17.8	18.4	−0.6	44.9
1962	17.6	18.8	−1.3	43.7
1963	17.8	18.6	−0.8	42.4
1964	17.6	18.5	−0.9	40.1
1965	17.0	17.2	−0.2	38.0
1966	17.4	17.9	−0.5	35.0
1967	18.3	19.4	−1.1	32.8
1968	17.6	20.5	−2.9	33.4
1969	19.7	19.4	+0.3	29.3
1970	19.1	19.4	−0.3	28.1
1971	17.4	19.5	−2.1	28.1
1972	17.6	19.6	−2.0	27.4
1973	17.7	18.8	−1.1	26.1
1974	18.3	18.7	−0.4	23.9
1975	18.0	21.4	−3.4	25.4
1976	17.2	21.5	−4.3	27.6
1977	18.0	20.8	−2.7	27.9
1978	18.1	20.7	−2.7	27.4
1979	18.6	20.2	−1.6	25.7
1980	19.0	21.7	−2.7	26.1
1981	19.7	22.2	−2.6	25.8
1982	19.2	23.2	−4.0	28.6
1983	17.6	23.6	−6.1	33.1
1984	17.5	22.3	−4.9	34.1
1985	17.9	23.1	−5.2	36.6
1986	17.6	22.6	−5.1	39.7
1987	18.6	21.8	−3.3	41.0
1988	18.4	21.5	−3.1	41.4
1989	18.5	21.4	−2.8	40.9
1990	18.2	22.0	−3.9	42.4
1991	18.0	22.6	−4.6	45.9
1992	17.8	22.5	−4.7	48.8
1993	17.8	21.8	−3.9	50.2
1994	18.4	21.4	−3.0	50.2
1995	18.8	21.1	−2.3	50.1
1996	19.4	20.8	−1.4	49.9

Source: Economic Report of the President, February 1997, Table B–77, p. 390.

APPENDIX

I believe that NUBAR is worth enacting because the rule imposes some discipline on legislators without the risk of turning a recession into a depression. But some economists have criticisms of any balanced budget rule, even NUBAR. Here are some points they've made.

"The rule should set a target for government saving, not for the government budget." This accusation has merit. Prepare for some exciting, inescapable accounting. National saving is the sum of private saving plus government saving. If our goal is raising national saving, our target should be raising government saving. But what is government saving? Saving is defined as net income minus consumption, so government saving equals government net income (taxes minus transfers such as Social Security benefit payments) minus government consumption purchases of goods and services. Imagine you're the government treasurer. If taxes increase $100 billion or transfers are cut $100 billion, then "your" (government) saving increases $100 billion. What matters for national saving is government saving, so the rule should set a target for taxes minus transfers minus government consumption purchases. Note that government investment purchases should be ignored.

But balancing the budget means counting government investment purchases. The government surplus (which we call a "deficit" when it is negative) is defined as government net income (taxes minus transfers) minus *all* government purchases—for investment as well as consumption. If our aim is to raise national saving, then the ideal rule would be a target for government saving, not the government surplus or deficit. Government saving is not increased if government purchases for investment—highways, bridges, dams, and so forth—are cut, even though this helps to reduce the government deficit and balance the budget.

There is, however, a serious practical problem with a government saving rule. Government investment must be distinguished from government consumption. This is no easy task in many cases. Legislators would have a strong incentive to define any government purchase as investment, so that the purchase can be made despite the government saving target.

A balanced budget rule puts pressure on taxes, transfers, and government purchases for consumption; this pressure raises government saving and hence national saving. But it also puts downward pressure on government purchases for investment, and this pressure has no effect on government saving.

Is the pressure on government investment desirable? If the return on government investment exceeds the return on private investment, then the pressure would be undesirable. But if government investment yields a lower return than private investment, then the pressure is desirable, because it would be better if a greater fraction of national saving was directed toward the private sector.

But it is difficult to measure the return on government investment. For example, consider a highway. A private firm would try to maximize revenue by its toll structure. But government often does not try to maximize toll revenue. Thus, the return on this government investment, measured by toll revenue, is less than the return a private firm would achieve. In this case, the measured return understates the social return on the investment.

On the other hand, notorious "pork barrel" projects often have a low return, but they are politically profitable to individual legislators. It would clearly be desirable to have the promoters of these projects feel pressure from a balanced budget rule.

So it is unclear whether a balanced budget rule applies the right degree of pressure to government investment. But the pressure it applies to taxes, transfers, and government consumption spending tends to raise the national saving rate. The best should not be an excuse to prevent the good.

"The government deficit is measured incorrectly." The charge has merit, but does not undermine the case for NUBAR. Why?

Suppose a conventionally measured deficit of $50 billion implies a properly measured deficit of $0. If NUBAR uses conventional measurement, it would require a shift in the budget to achieve a conventionally measured planned budget deficit of $0, which might imply a properly measured surplus of $50 billion. Is this undesirable?

If the goal were to balance the correctly measured budget, aiming at conventionally measured balance would obviously be undesirable. But if the goal is to impose discipline on legislators and to raise the national saving rate above its current level, then aiming at conventionally measured balance is still desirable. As long as reducing the conventional deficit generally corresponds to raising national saving, then the rule is desirable, despite measurement error.

"Raising government saving does not always raise national saving." This assertion is theoretically correct, because it is possible for the increase in government saving to induce an offsetting reduction in private saving. For example, suppose there were no Social Security system, and that individuals saved privately for retirement. Now suppose Social Security is enacted, but unlike our actual system, it is to be financed like a properly run private pension. When the system is introduced, workers are taxed, but no benefits are paid, so that a genuine fund accumulates. Then as each worker retires, he draws down the fund he has built by tax contributions (plus interest).

In the first years after enactment, the Social Security tax raises revenue, but there is no government spending, so government saving increases, and the government deficit—including the Social Security account—is reduced. But there may be no increase in national saving. Why? Because individuals may cut their private saving by an amount equal to the government saving done on their behalf. For example, for each $100 of additional payroll tax, a worker may cut his private saving $100, because he views his payroll tax as a form of saving. Thus, some forms of government saving may trigger a corresponding cut in private saving.

But this Social Security example is the exception rather than the rule. In general, there will be much less than a full private offset when government saving increases. For example, suppose there is a household tax increase, and government spending is held constant. But in contrast to the Social Security case, the tax revenue is not earmarked for any specific purpose or fund. There is no particular reason why individuals should regard the tax as a substitute for private saving. Also, the tax increase is not intended to be temporary, so there is no reason for individuals to view it as a one-year aberration. Thus, there is no reason to expect individuals to cut private saving nearly as much as the increase in government saving.

Suppose a household's tax rises $1,000, but the government promises no additional future transfer, in contrast to the Social Security case. Then it is likely that much of the tax will come out of the household's consumption, so that private saving will fall much less than $1,000. In the United States, the personal saving rate is roughly 5 percent; out of every $1,000 of current after-tax income, the average household consumes $950 and saves $50. Suppose the tax causes consumption to fall $950 and private saving to fall $50. Then when government saving rises $1,000, private saving falls only $50, so that national saving rises by $950—95 percent of the tax increase. As long as private saving falls less than $1,000, national saving will increase.

Let us summarize our response to the objections. Each has merit. A NUBAR statute must plead guilty to the charge of imperfection. But the quest for the best must not be allowed to prevent achievement of the good. Despite these objections, it remains true that a NUBAR statute will raise the national saving rate without destabilizing the economy, and impose some fiscal discipline on Congress and the president. That should be good enough for practical reformers.

6 STABILIZING THE ECONOMY

What do I mean by "stabilizing the economy?"

I'm sure you'll agree that it's nice when the unemployment rate stays "stable" and normal from year to year. An economy prone to sharp rises in the unemployment rate is unpleasant, not only for the people who are laid off, but also for everyone who worries that he may be laid off. An unstable unemployment rate spells immediate hardship for some and prolonged anxiety for many. You'll recall that a severe problem along these lines developed in the 1930s. The catastrophe of the Great Depression, with roughly 25 percent of the labor force unemployed at its trough, sent economists back to the drawing board and gave birth to modern macroeconomics, launched by the pathbreaking book by Cambridge University's John Maynard Keynes entitled *The General Theory of Employment, Interest, and Money* (1936). The theme of that book was why an economic depression can occur, why it won't automatically cure itself, and how government policy can prevent it from happening, and cure it if it does.

Also, you'll surely acknowledge that it's nice when prices are relatively "stable"—in other words, when the economy has little or no inflation. At the end of the 1970s, over the course of a year, the average price rose roughly 10 percent—too fast for most people. Of course, many countries experience much higher inflation rates. In the 1990s, inflation has been about 3 percent in the United States. So by "stabilization" I mean keeping unemployment normal and without major fluctuations, and inflation low.

So whose job is it to stabilize the economy? Maybe the best way to arrive at an answer is to look at a stabilization achievement of the early 1980s—*disinflation* (the reduction in inflation). Recall that time. A stubborn 10 percent inflation was widely declared to be public enemy number one. Yet in less than half a decade, inflation had been cut more than in half and was no longer considered a serious problem. Who brought inflation down?

Whodunit

In 1979, with the inflation rate near 10 percent, President Carter appointed Paul Volcker to be chairman of the central bank of the United States—the Federal Reserve. Volcker and his colleagues resolved to do what was necessary to bring down inflation. They applied a "tight money" policy to the economy, long enough and hard enough, until the resulting severe recession brought down inflation.

Let's go through that more slowly. I'll explain what "tight money" means in a minute. But first, why does a deep recession bring down inflation? A deep recession means layoffs. Many workers become alarmed that they will lose their jobs. So instead of being aggressive at the bargaining table, unions are willing to make concessions to save jobs. Not only that, the recession also means poor profits, and employers simply can't afford large wage increases. So a deep recession slowly brings down wage increases.

Business firms set price increases to cover cost increases. When wage increases get smaller, business firms can afford to reduce price increases. And competition forces them to. Also, in a recession, market demand won't support customary price increases. So price increases get smaller. Hence, inflation declines.

The members of the Fed knew that disinflation would not be a very pleasant process. I'm sure they undertook their assignment with great regret. But there is no escaping the central point. The Fed can bring down inflation only by generating a recession. And that's precisely what it did at the beginning of the 1980s.

How did the Fed do it? By making money "tight." What does this mean? The Fed raised interest rates high enough to discourage many households and businesses from borrowing. These households and businesses were forced to cut their spending on goods and services. When producers confronted the fall in demand, they had no choice but to cut production and lay off workers.

But how does the Fed raise interest rates? Every month, unbeknownst to most of the public, the Federal Reserve's Open Market Committee—the FOMC—meets in Washington. The FOMC consists of the Fed chairman (currently Alan Greenspan, who replaced Paul Volcker), six other board members who have been appointed by the president (each term is fourteen years), and several Fed regional bank presidents. They are advised by an excellent staff of well-trained economists.

Each month the FOMC decides the stance of monetary policy— to tighten or to loosen, that is the monthly question. At the beginning of the 1980s, the FOMC almost always resolved to tighten. It told the Fed manager of *open market operations* in New York to cut down the purchase of government bonds. Let's see how this decision raised interest rates in the economy.

When the Fed buys bonds, the seller—a household, business firm, or governmental unit—deposits the check in its bank. The bank, in turn, obtains cash from the Fed to cover the check. Now you might think that the bank had better hold on to this cash, because, after all, it really belongs to the depositor, who could come in any old time and ask for it. But centuries ago, an early banker experienced the ecstasy of discovering that his depositors would never know if he lent out part of their cash. And by lending it, he could earn interest. So he did. And so have banks ever since.

So whenever a bank enjoys an infusion of cash, it immediately tries to lend out part of it. The more cash it has, the lower the

Table 6.1

	Unemployment rate (%)	Prime interest rate (%)	Inflation rate (%)
1977	6.9	6.83	6.7
1978	6.0	9.06	7.3
1979	5.8	12.67	8.9
1980	7.0	15.27	9.0
1981	7.5	18.87	9.7
1982	9.5	14.86	6.4
1983	9.5	10.79	3.8

interest rate the bank must offer to get potential borrowers to take all of it. So when the Fed cut down its purchase of government bonds at the beginning of the 1980s, less cash flowed into banks. With less cash, banks could charge a high interest rate and still find enough borrowers for their limited supply of cash.

By cutting down its purchase of bonds, the Fed raised interest rates throughout the economy. Each month the FOMC would ask: Have we tightened enough? The question was easy to answer. If there was still no recession, then more tightening was necessary. Table 6.1 shows what the Fed was doing: Each month, the FOMC would observe the unemployment rate. If it was still in the 6.5 percent range, then the Fed would take the interest rate up, wait a month, then observe again. The borrowers and spenders in the economy held out gallantly as the prime rate (the interest rate banks charge their most favored customers) rose to unprecedented heights. Finally, in late 1981, the Fed won its battle, and many potential borrowers and spenders surrendered. Confronted with record interest rates, they at last cut down their borrowing and spending. The economy fell off a cliff into the worst recession since the 1930s as the unemployment rate rose sharply in 1982. In the worst month of 1982, the unemployment rate nearly reached 11 percent, and it averaged 9.5 percent for the year.

Table 6.1 also shows that the severe recession succeeded in bringing down inflation. Just in time, in mid-1982 the Fed relented, let interest rates come down, and prevented the recession from becoming a depression. In fact, a recovery began in 1983 (though it was still not evident in the unemployment rate), and was running at full steam in 1984. Since then, the Fed has done a good job of keeping the unemployment rate near normal and the inflation rate low. There was a mild recession in the early 1990s, but the unemployment rate never approached 8 percent. By the mid-1990s, the unemployment rate was below 5.5 percent and the inflation rate was about 2 percent.

Should the Fed have done it? Most economists agree that inflation had to be brought down. Some would have preferred a milder recession that lasted longer to the sharp, severe recession that occurred. But most concede that it is difficult for the Fed to fine-tune a slowdown of the economy. It is possible that most FOMC members would also have preferred a milder, longer recession.

Could the Fed have used any help? A minority of economists think a wage-price policy could have helped the Fed bring down inflation with less recession by applying some direct pressure to firms to reduce price increases. The majority of economists disagree and think a wage-price policy would have been ineffective. In any case, it's now water under the bridge. Inflation is down, and almost all economists agree that it's up to the Fed to keep it that way.

So let's summarize: The Fed intentionally caused the recession of 1982 and the reduction in inflation that accompanied it. The two went together. Without the recession, there would have been no disinflation. And the Fed generated both.

Miseducation by Politicians

But you would never know "whodunit" if you listened to the rhetoric of the two political conventions of 1984. The Republicans praised President Reagan for conquering inflation but regarded the recession of 1982 as an irrelevant natural disaster, akin to an earthquake. The Democrats blamed the president for causing the worst recession since the 1930s but regarded the disinflation as a mysterious natural blessing, akin to a fortuitous change in the climate. Economists could only sit in front of their

TV sets and watch helplessly as millions of Americans were miseducated about recent economic history. How had inflation been brought down? The Republicans cheerfully told the media, "The president's policies." Which policies, exactly? The media (with a few exceptions) never asked, and the Republicans never said.

Well, that's not quite true. The best of the Republicans never said, because they knew that talking about the Fed's recession was not likely to win votes, so rather than distort any further, they just repeated, "The president's policies," and left it at that. Unfortunately, there were other Republicans who went further. They said, "The president's historic tax cut brought down inflation."

Now, the temptation is understandable. After all, to the general public, the president's most famous economic policy was surely the income tax cut he proposed, and persuaded Congress to enact, in 1981. So why. not claim that the tax cut did it? Indeed, such a claim would be widely believed for the unfortunate reason that most of the public has not had the opportunity to study any economics.

But few things drive economists wilder than the claim that the tax cut of 1981 brought down inflation. If you took a survey of economists of all political persuasions, there would be near unanimity that it was the tight money policy of the Fed that generated both the severe recession and the resulting reduction in inflation. Don't misunderstand. Many (though not all) conservative economists supported the tax cut of 1981. But not to bring down inflation. For example, Milton Friedman, dean of "monetarist" economists, supported the tax cut because, as a conservative, he wanted to reduce the size of government. But Friedman, who has devoted much of his career to emphasizing the importance of money in the determination of inflation, would be near apoplexy should someone claim that the tax cut of 1981 brought down inflation.

Now what about the Democrats? They claimed that "Reaganomics" had caused the worst recession since the 1930s. But which policies, exactly? They never said. Well, once again, that's not quite true. The best of the Democrats never said, because then it would come out that the Fed did it to reduce inflation. And worse yet, they would have to admit that their own president, Jimmy Carter, had appointed Volcker Fed chairman in 1979, so that if any president was indirectly responsible, it was a Democratic president. So the best of the Democrats just said, "Reaganomics," and let it go at that.

But unfortunately, some Democrats went further. Once again, the temptation is understandable. Since President Reagan's most famous economic policy was his tax cut, these Democrats hinted that the president's tax cut caused the worst recession since the 1930s. Few could get themselves to literally say that the tax cut caused the recession. But they would say, "The tax cut was a great mistake. Look what happened. We got the worst recession since the 1930s." Now, if there is anything that drives economists wilder than the claim that the tax cut brought down inflation, it is the claim that the tax cut caused the recession. How in God's name can a tax cut cause a recession? A tax cut leaves more cash in people's pockets and raises their spending on goods and services, thereby stimulating production and employment—the opposite of recession.

As for the 1982 recession, there is also a small timing problem. The tax cut was enacted in 1981 to be phased in over 1982 and 1983. But the economy plunged into recession before the tax cut took full effect. In fact, the tax cut contributed to the recovery that began in 1983 as a result of the Fed's shifting gears in mid-1982.

So why were the politicians of both parties able to mislead the public? While our nation certainly has some reporters with excellent training in economics, unfortunately many reporters who cover politics have not had the opportunity to study economics, and naturally shy away from asking questions like, "Mr. Republican, exactly how did the tax cut reduce inflation?" or "Mr. Democrat, exactly how did Reaganomics cause the recession?"

The Fed's Target

What must the Fed do to stabilize the economy, to keep unemployment and inflation on target and relatively constant? Before answering this question, we must check something immediately. Are our two goals compatible? If unemployment is on target, will inflation stay constant?

Experience over the past three decades seems to suggest that if the U.S. economy is run near a particular unemployment rate—about 5.5 percent currently—then the inflation rate usually stays roughly constant. If the unemployment rate is much below this particular value, then inflation usually rises; and if the unemployment rate is much above this particular value, then inflation usually falls. For example, in the late 1960s, the unemployment rate was near 4 percent, and inflation rose. In the 1982 recession, the unemployment rate exceeded 9 percent, and inflation declined, as we saw in Table 6.1.

So if we accept the hypothesis that the economy has a *constant-inflation* unemployment rate, or CIRU (pronounced "see-roo"), and if we accept this CIRU as our unemployment rate target, then our two goals are compatible. Incidentally, many economists call the CIRU the *natural rate of unemployment.* I prefer *CIRU,* to emphasize the point that if the economy is at this unemployment rate, the inflation rate usually stays constant. Other economists call it the NAIRU (non-accelerating inflation rate of unemployment). But *constant* is clearer than *non-accelerating,* so I prefer CIRU. At any rate, if you read an article that talks about the natural rate of unemployment or the NAIRU, the author means the same thing as I mean by CIRU.

There is considerable uncertainty about the numerical value of the CIRU. During most of the 1980s, the CIRU appeared to be near 6.5 percent. Today, it may be closer to 5.5 percent. I will use the value 5.5 percent in my examples.

Why does inflation usually rise if the economy is below the CIRU? A low unemployment rate raises the relative bargaining strength of workers. The fear of layoffs diminishes, and unions become more aggressive. Employers have difficulty finding workers and are afraid of losing workers through stingy wage increases. Moreover, a low unemployment rate usually means that businesses are enjoying high revenues and profits, so they can afford higher wage increases. Thus, a low unemployment rate usually results in a rise in wage increases, cost increases, and price increases—that is, a rise in inflation.

Just the reverse is true if the economy has a high unemployment rate. A high unemployment rate reduces the relative bargaining strength of workers. The fear of layoffs rises, and unions become more timid. Employers have no difficulty finding workers, and have no fear of losing workers through stingy wage increases. Moreover, a high unemployment rate usually means that businesses are suffering low revenues and profits, so they are forced to reduce wage increases. Thus, a high unemployment rate usually results in a fall in wage increases, cost increases, and price increases—a fall in inflation.

Imagine for a moment that inflation is zero and unemployment is at the CIRU—roughly 5.5 percent. How can the Fed keep it that way? If output per worker—labor productivity—grows 2 percent per year due to capital accumulation and technological change, then the same number of workers can produce 2 percent more output next year. So if real output grows 2 percent, the unemployment rate will stay at 5.5 percent if the labor force—the number who want to work—remains constant. If the labor force grows 0.5 percent instead of staying constant, then real output must grow 2.5 percent to keep the unemployment rate at 5.5 percent. I will call the sum of productivity growth and labor force growth *normal real output growth*. In this example, normal real output growth is therefore 2.5 percent (2 percent plus 0.5 percent).

Suppose the Fed chooses an ambitious goal of 0 percent inflation. Then the Fed's job is to make total dollar spending in the economy rise 2.5 percent per year. If it does, there will be enough demand to buy 2.5 percent more real output, since 0 percent is needed for price increases. If real output rises 2.5 percent, then the unemployment rate will stay at 5.5 percent. And if the unemployment rate is 5.5 percent, then experience shows that inflation should stay steady; if the inflation rate was 0 percent last year, it should stay 0 percent this year.

So if the Fed wants a zero-inflation economy with the unemployment rate at the CIRU, it must try to keep the growth rate of total spending equal to normal real output growth—2.5 percent in this example. However, the Fed may be less ambitious. It may settle for a steady 2 percent inflation rate. If so, then its task is to keep the growth rate of total spending at 4.5 percent, so that 2 percent of the spending goes for price increases, and 2.5 percent for an increase in real output.

Why might the Fed accept a 2 percent goal for inflation, rather than 0 percent? If inflation is 2 percent then unit cost growth must be 2 percent; if productivity growth is 2 percent, then the *average* wage increase must be 4 percent. Some wage increases are above 4 percent, and some are below 4 percent, but very few wage "increases" are negative—an actual cut in the dollar amount of the wage. But if inflation is 0 percent then unit cost growth must be 0 percent; so the *average* wage increase must be 2 percent. Some wage increases are above 2 percent, some are below 2 percent, and quite a few wage "increases" are negative. But many workers especially resent actual cuts in the dollar amount of the wage. Such cuts may reduce morale and productivity or cause some workers to quit rather than accept what they regard as an insult. The result might be lower productivity and a rise in the CIRU. Thus, it may be better to accept an inflation goal of 2 percent, with an average wage increase of 4 percent, and very few actual cuts in the dollar amount of any wage.

We can summarize: The Fed's target is to achieve a growth rate of total spending equal to normal real output growth plus the desired inflation rate. Since normal real output growth is roughly 2.5 percent, if the Fed accepts an inflation goal of 2 percent, then the Fed's normal target should be a growth rate of total spending of about 4.5 percent.

The Great Offsetter

How can the Fed meet its target for total spending growth? The answer is that the Fed is the great offsetter. Its job is to assess the other forces influencing total spending in the economy and to lean against the wind.

Suppose the Fed estimates that household and business psychology, and government budget policy, will all tend to make spending grow too slowly in the months ahead. Then the Fed's job is to stimulate spending. How? By reducing interest rates. How? By injecting more cash into the banking system. How? By buying more government bonds in the open market.

Recall again how this works. When the Fed buys government bonds, the sellers—households, businesses, and governmental units—deposit Fed checks at their banks. The banks, in turn, obtain cash from the Fed to cover the checks. The banks then seek borrowers so that they can earn interest on part of this cash. The more bonds the Fed buys, the more cash the banks obtain, and the lower the interest rate they must offer to induce potential borrowers to take all the cash they seek to lend.

So to stimulate more borrowing and spending in the economy, the Fed simply raises its *open market* purchases of government bonds. It does just the reverse if it wants to reduce the growth of spending in the economy.

Of course, hitting it just right is no simple task. I don't want to give the false impression that the Fed can fine-tune the growth of total spending. After all, it's hard to guess at consumer and business psychology. Currently, it's difficult to guess what government budget policy will be. And even if the Fed knew these precisely, it could not be sure exactly how much to adjust its bond purchases because the link between money injection and the fall in interest rates and rise in spending is imprecise.

So we can't expect perfection from the Fed. But the Fed is often able to do a pretty good job. Its excellent technical staff uses the best econometric models—economic models based on statistical analysis of U.S. economic data—to try to estimate the bond purchases that will keep total spending growth on target. And it continuously adjusts its open market operations based on new data.

The Fed has controlled the economy fairly well since the deep recession of 1982. Remember, it intentionally engineered the 1982 recession in order to bring down inflation. Since then it has kept spending growth near its target, so that the unemployment rate has stayed near 5.5 percent, real output growth has stayed near 2.5 percent, and the inflation rate has stayed steady below 3 percent.

However, the Fed has done better in some years than in others. Under the leadership of its new chairman, Alan Greenspan (appointed by President Reagan), it handled the stock market crash of October 1987 very nicely, so that the economic recovery was hardly interrupted. The Fed missed at the beginning of the 1990s, and there was a mild recession, with the unemployment rate rising from 5.6 percent in 1990 to 6.8 percent in 1991 to a peak of 7.5 percent in 1992. This was much milder than the intentional recession of 1982, with a peak unemployment rate of 9.5 percent that lasted two years. But it was severe enough to help defeat President Bush in his bid for re-election in 1992. Since then, the Fed has gradually reduced the unemployment rate to below 5.5 percent in 1996 without generating any upward move in inflation in 1996. This excellent performance undoubtedly contributed to the re-election of President Clinton in 1996. The Fed and its chairman cannot forecast perfectly—nor can anyone else—so they can't prevent mild fluctuations in the economy. But they have a very good chance to prevent severe recessions or severe rises in inflation.

Suppose we phase in a policy that raises household saving. For example, we gradually convert from the income tax to the consumption tax as described in chapter 3. What must the Fed do? The Fed should anticipate a slowdown in the growth of consumer spending. It must therefore act in advance to reduce interest rates in order to stimulate investment spending. As the policy phases in, the Fed should raise its purchase of government bonds, injecting more cash into the banking system, and the result will be a fall in interest rates and a rise in borrowing by business firms to finance investment in plants and equipment.

Thus, the Fed must offset the slower growth in consumer spending by stimulating faster growth in investment spending. If the Fed hits it just right, the result will be to keep total spending growth on target. But the composition of this growth will have been changed to faster investment growth and slower consumption growth.

This may strike some readers as a delicate operation. It is. But it is no more delicate than the one the Fed performs every day. Whether we implement our policy or not, the economy is continuously subject to changes in spending that the Fed must offset in order to keep it stable. The Fed's job is to be the great offsetter, and it usually performs its job remarkably well.

Should the President and Congress Try to Help?

The president and Congress have plenty to do. There's no danger that they will wilt offstage if they leave stabilization to the Fed. And "leave it to the Fed" is just what they should do, except when a severe recession creates an economic emergency.

Actually, there is one step the president and Congress can take when it comes to stabilization. They can avoid destabilizing fiscal actions that make the Fed's job much tougher. The best way to do this is to lock themselves into neutrality and predictability by enacting the normal unemployment balanced budget rule (NUBAR) described in chapter 5. Recall that the goal of NUBAR is modest. It keeps the federal budget neutral. It prevents shifts in the budget that would make a recession or inflation worse. It prevents destabilization due to government fiscal (budget) policy.

NUBAR would also make government fiscal policy predictable. At last, the Fed would know what the federal budget position would be. And this would make it easier for the Fed to conduct an effective monetary policy. The Fed still could not be sure what the private sector's spending would be. But at least it would have a better idea about government spending and taxes.

Now, why shouldn't the president and Congress be more ambitious? Why shouldn't they try to actively stabilize the economy rather than simply adhering to a rule such as NUBAR and leaving the Fed to do the rest? True, the president and Congress have the power to raise and lower spending in the economy. The Fed does it by moving interest rates. The president and Congress could do it by changing the taxes people pay, or by changing the government's own spending. In theory, the president and Congress could even stabilize the economy without the Fed's help.

The problem is not with theory, but with practice. Two historical examples will make my point. In the early 1960s, many economists believed that the unemployment rate was unnecessarily high, and that a tax cut should be used to stimulate the economy. So a tax cut was enacted and, along with an expansionary monetary policy, it helped reduce the unemployment rate. But in the mid-1960s, the buildup in military spending for the Vietnam War resulted in excessive spending, thereby threatening to push the unemployment rate below the CIRU, and raise inflation.

In theory, the answer was simple. Just as the president and Congress had stimulated private spending by cutting taxes, now they must restrain spending by raising taxes. In theory, symmetry was easy. But in practice, it was not. The chairman of the Council of Economic Advisers, Gardiner Ackley, told President Johnson that a tax increase was required to prevent inflation. President Johnson, however, decided that the last thing he needed was to ask the American people for a tax increase to help finance the military buildup. So he delayed for two years, and by then inflation had already risen substantially.

Now to my second example, which we've already discussed. At the beginning of the 1980s, the country cried out for disinflation. The Fed rose to the challenge and applied the painful medicine of a tight money recession until disinflation was achieved. Now what did the president and Congress do during this period when the economy badly needed restraint?

You guessed it. They enacted a sweeping tax cut and raised spending as a fraction of GDP, thereby stimulating the economy. Luckily, their brave actions hit the economy after the Fed had generated the deep recession and disinflation, so that the fiscal stimulus helped fuel the recovery. But to credit them with wisdom, rather than luck, would be ludicrous.

Let me put it this way. Suppose it had been up to Congress and the president alone to generate the recession and disinflation. Suppose we had relied on them to get the job done by raising taxes and cutting spending enough to slow total spending in the economy. Is there any doubt that they would have failed and our inflation problem would have persisted or even gotten worse?

So what lessons should we draw from these episodes? Some economists conclude that we should redouble our efforts to teach politicians to practice symmetrical fiscal policy. They must be taught to vote promptly for tax increases and spending cuts when the economy needs slower spending. But I draw another conclusion. Let's face it: Congressmen and senators are never going to go cheerfully on record voting for tax increases and spending cuts, and few presidents propose such austerity in the first place. If they are willing to do so at all, it is after months of delay. So if we let them vote every few months, they will inevitably practice asymmetrical policy. They may cut taxes and raise spending when we ask for stimulus (though probably after months of debate and delay), but they will strangely lose their ability to hear us when we call for restraint.

By contrast, the Fed can engineer restraint when restraint is needed. Why? Not because the Fed is necessarily wiser than Congress and the president, but because it is more insulated from political and popular pressure. First of all, much of the public has never heard of the Fed. How many people understand how the Fed influences the fluctuations of the economy? Second, the members of the Fed Open Market Committee don't run for office every two, four, or six years.

Consider this scene from mid-1982. It's a dinner party in suburban Washington, D.C. But instead of cheer, there is gloom and tension around the table. As one guest empties his wineglass for the sixth time, he whispers to his neighbor that his business is about to go under, ruined by the worst recession since the 1930s.

"That son of a——in the White House will never get my vote again. And the whole damned Congress should be drowned in the Potomac," he mutters in anguish. Then he asks his neighbor, "And what do you do?"

"I'm a banker," comes the reply. All around the dinner table, denunciations of the president and Congress can be heard. One man has lost his job, but no one knows it. Several others fear for theirs. Only the banker seems calm.

With good reason. Not only is his job secure, but no one at the dinner party knows is that he is no ordinary banker. In fact, he has been a member of the Fed's Open Market Committee for several years. His monthly votes have generated the recession that has caused the immediate pain around the table. The resulting disinflation will set the stage for a strong recovery that will last for the rest of the decade. But the pleasure of that recovery is still in the future. Perhaps as he voted, he was strengthened by the knowledge that no one in his social circle would ever know his role or responsibility.

Now, anyone who believes in democracy must have mixed feelings about such a dinner party scene. It is troubling that symmetrical stabilization policy, necessary for the long-run health of the economy, seems to depend on insulation from popular and political pressure. But after all, isn't this the reason we try to insulate the Supreme Court?

So we have two choices. We can exhort Congress and the president to be courageous, and count on them to vote for fiscal medicine when it is medicine we need; or we can face political reality and be thankful that we have another option, to count on the Fed.

If we decide to count on the Fed, then what should we want from Congress and the president? Simply, that they tie their own hands so they can't do harm. They can do this by obeying NUBAR. Every year, Congress should enact a planned budget for the coming fiscal year that technicians estimate will be balanced if next year's unemployment rate is normal (the average of the preceding decade). So my request to Congress and the president is simply this: Enact a NUBAR statute, obey it, and then leave stabilization to the Fed, except in the emergency of a severe recession.

A Division of Labor

So who should try to keep the unemployment rate near the current CIRU, and inflation steady and low? Our good old central bank, the Federal Reserve. What should the president and Congress do about stabilization? Enact a normal unemployment balanced budget rule (NUBAR) and obey it. Then leave stabilization to the Fed, except in the emergency of a severe recession. If each sticks to its proper assignment, the whole job can be nicely done.

7 INTERNATIONAL TRADE

This is a tale of two islands: Labor Land and Capital Land. The islands were separated by a sea, and before the invention of ships, neither knew of the other's existence. In fact, each thought it was the only land on earth.

Whatever the reason, most Labor Landers never accumulated much capital—physical, knowledge, or human capital. Yes, most learned how to make some simple tools, grow a few crops, build simple houses, and read, write, and do arithmetic. But that was all. Naturally, their productivity, wage, and standard of living were low. However, a few Labor Landers owned machines and were highly educated and trained; naturally, their productivity, wage, and standard of living were high.

Things were very different in Capital Land. Capital Landers invented productive machines and discovered how to make many products. Most were highly educated and trained. Naturally, their productivity, wage, and standard of living were high. However, some Capital Landers failed to own capital and obtain much education and training. A few were simply lazy, but others, despite their best efforts, were unable to learn advanced skills. Naturally, their productivity, wage, and standard of living were low.

One day there was great excitement at a huge factory located on the Capital Land seashore. A huge object, constructed in the factory, was being towed into the water. A crowd of people gathered to watch.

"It's going to sink, it's going to sink!" shouted a little boy. But it didn't sink. To the disbelief of children and adults alike, it floated. A cheer arose from the workers in the factory, then another from the crowd. The factory manager climbed up a ladder on the outside of the object, then stepped over a railing, stood on a deck inside the object, and addressed the crowd.

"We've done it. I am proud to announce that all of you are witnessing a historic moment: the launching of the first ship. For thousands of years we have stared at the sea that surrounds our island. Now at last we will be able to discover if we are truly alone on earth."

One week later a brave crew set sail at dawn. As a crowd watched, the ship sailed slowly into the distance. As night fell the ship could no longer be seen. The next morning it was gone.

"I can't see it anymore," said a little girl. "Did it sink?"

"We don't know," answered her mother. "They have enough food to sail for a month. They've been given orders to turn back in two weeks. Let us pray for them."

Exactly one month later a cheering crowd greeted the returning ship. The sailors hurried down the ladders, bursting with excitement.

"We discovered another populated island!" they shouted. "The people were friendly as can be. We're going to trade, we're going to trade!"

"What does 'trade' mean?" asked a little girl.

"It means," a sailor replied, "that we'll exchange some products we've made for some products they've made."

Comparative Advantage

"Why should we trade?" asked Autarkas. "Do they make anything that we can't make?" The sailors were suddenly quiet. Finally one sailor admitted, "I didn't see any product we can't make. You see, most Labor Landers have little machinery, education, and training. Most of our workers, equipped with advanced machines, education, and training, can out-produce them in every product. I'll give you two examples. First, consider a product we are most proud of: hitech [pronounced 'high teck']."

"Can Labor Landers even make a hitech?" asked Autarkas.

"This may surprise you," replied the sailor. "They actually manage to produce a small quantity of hitechs. But it's pitiful. One of our workers can produce 10 times as many hitechs in the same time as one of their workers can."

"What's your second example?" asked Autarkas.

"It's the product lotech [pronounced 'low teck']," replied the sailor. "Lotech doesn't require a lot of machinery, education, and training to produce, so the Labor Landers do a lot better making lotechs than they do making hitechs."

"But," persisted Autarkas, "can one of their workers beat one of our workers at making a lotech?"

"Well," conceded the sailor, "not really. One of our workers can produce 5 times as many lotechs in the same time as one of theirs can."

"So," said Autarkas with a satisfied smile, "we have an *absolute* advantage in every product. Our advantage is 10 times for hitechs and 5 times for lotechs. So again, I repeat, why trade? We're better off making every product ourselves."

Just then there was a disturbance in the crowd as a young, well-dressed gentleman made his way to the front until he stood facing Autarkas and the sailor.

"Autarkas, what you say sounds so sensible," the young gentleman said. "At first glance it surely seems pointless to trade with Labor Land when we have an absolute advantage in every product. But, alas, what seems sensible at first glance does not always turn out to be true on deeper analysis. That analysis shows that Capital Land and Labor Land can both gain from specializing in production and then trading freely."

"Who are you?" asked Autarkas.

"I'm Ricardo," the young gentleman replied.

"I've heard of you," said Autarkas. "You made a fortune as a stockbroker as a very young man, and now you serve in our legislature. You are certainly a successful, practical man. So how can you think trading with Labor Land makes sense for us?"

"You were kind enough to note my practical successes. But you may not be aware that two years ago I published a treatise on political economy, the result of many hours of analysis and work. In one chapter of my treatise I explained why free trade would make both lands better off."

"But this is quite remarkable," said Autarkas. "How could you even write about trade with another land in your treatise? We just discovered the existence of Labor Land, and your treatise was published two years ago!"

"I have two answers," replied Ricardo. "First, the idea that specializing and trading is mutually beneficial applies to a single land, two lands, or many lands. Second, I admit that in my treatise chapter I did assume that there were two lands. But you see, I can assume what I want. I'm an economist."

"If you are really an economist, you are quite right: You can assume anything. But why will we gain from free trade with Labor Land?" repeated Autarkas.

"Sailor," asked Ricardo, "how many lotechs does one Labor Lander produce in a day?"

"He produces 4," replied the sailor, "while one of us produces 20 in a day. As I said before, we're 5 times as productive as they are in lotechs."

"And how many hitechs does one Labor Lander produce in a day?" asked Ricardo.

"Just 1," answered the sailor, "while one of us produces 10 in a day. As I said before, we're 10 times as productive as they are in hitechs."

"So let's produce both hitechs and lotechs ourselves," said Autarkas.

"That would be a mistake," said Ricardo. "When one of our workers spends a day making lotechs instead of hitechs, he produces 20 lotechs instead of 10 hitechs. So our sacrifice of 10 hitechs gets us 20 lotechs to consume. Do you agree that it would be better if our worker spent the day making 10 hitechs and then traded the 10 hitechs for 30 lotechs from Labor Land?"

"Obviously," replied Autarkas. "Of course we'd rather have 30 lotechs at the end of the day than 20 lotechs. But will Labor Land agree to the trade?"

"They should," replied Ricardo. "When one of their workers spends ten days making hitechs instead of lotechs, he produces 10 hitechs instead of 40 lotechs. So he must sacrifice 40 lotechs to consume 10 hitechs. Wouldn't he be better off producing and trading only 30 lotechs to get 10 hitechs?"

"Indeed he would," answered Autarkas.

"Note this," said Ricardo. "Within Capital Land, the choice is 1 hitech or 2 lotechs, while within Labor Land, the choice is 1 hitech or 4 lotechs. It follows that if Capital Land can trade 1 hitech for more than 2 lotechs, it would gain; and if Labor Land can obtain 1 hitech for less than 4 lotechs, it would gain. So trade at any ratio between 1 to 2 and 1 to 4—for example, 1 to 3— would cause both lands to gain. With trade, Capital Land gets 3 lotechs for every hitech it sacrifices; without trade, it gets only 2. With trade, Labor Land gets 1 hitech for every 3 lotechs it sacrifices; without trade, it must sacrifice 4. That's why the trade of 10 hitechs from Capital Land for 30 lotechs from Labor Land (1 hitech for 3 lotechs) benefits both lands."

"That's simply remarkable," said an astonished Autarkas.

"It is indeed," said Ricardo. "I can't tell you how excited I was when I discovered it. If we are 10 times as productive as Labor Land in hitechs but only 5 times as productive as Labor Land in lotechs, then of course we have an absolute advantage in both goods. On average, we're 7.5 times as productive. But I propose to say that we have a *comparative* advantage in hitechs because our productivity multiple (10) is above average in hitechs, and Labor Land has a *comparative* advantage in lotechs because our productivity multiple (5) is below average in lotechs. We can both benefit if we each specialize in producing the good in which we have a comparative advantage, and then trading it."

"But the way you've defined comparative advantage," said Autarkas, "each land must have a comparative advantage in one of the two goods."

"Correct," replied Ricardo.

"So you are claiming that mutually beneficial trade is always possible, even when one land has an absolute advantage in all goods," said Autarkas.

"Exactly," replied Ricardo.

Free Trade

"But," said Autarkas, "you have not shown that free trade will actually benefit both lands. You've only shown that a mutually beneficial trade could be negotiated by planners, not that it would come about automatically in a free market."

"You are quite right," replied Ricardo. "So let me now demonstrate that in a free market, Capital Land will specialize in producing hitechs and export them and Labor Land will specialize in producing lotechs and export them, and these actions under a free market will result in both lands being better off."

"You've got quite a task," said Autarkas. "Labor Land uses money called labs, while we use money called caps. Their prices are in labs while ours are in caps. Before we can trade, we have to know what the exchange rate is between labs and caps. They want to sell me goods priced in labs and they want to be paid in labs. I need to know how many labs I can get at a bank for each cap—that is, I need to know the exchange rate—before I can figure out whether I need less caps to buy a lotech made in Labor Land than I would need to buy a lotech made in Capital Land. I need to know which source is cheaper. You're going to have to construct a very complicated numerical example, and while I might understand it, the crowd will never follow it."

"Not at all," replied Ricardo cheerfully. "I can do it without a numerical example. Suppose that at the initial prices and exchange rate, consumers in both lands would want to buy all their goods from Capital Land. In other words, when each consumer figures out which source is cheaper, it turns out that both goods made in Capital Land are cheaper."

"Sounds great," said Exportas, who had been listening to the whole discussion. "We'll be able to export hitechs and lotechs and make lots of money."

"You're a fool," interjected Importas, who was standing right next to him. "We'll be sending lots of goods to Labor Land for their people to consume, while all we'll get are pieces of paper called money."

"Actually," said Ricardo, "there's no point in you two getting into one of your famous arguments, because the situation won't last. If everyone tries to buy all goods from our producers, our prices and wages will rise, and if no one tries to buy goods from their producers, their prices and wages will fall."

"What will happen next?" asked the sailor.

"That's easy," replied Ricardo. "At some point, our rising prices and their falling prices will make one of our two goods more expensive. At that point, consumers will decide to buy that good from Labor Land, while still buying the other good from us because it's still cheaper. So the Labor Landers will specialize in making the first good, and we will specialize in making the second good."

"Which of our two goods will become more expensive?" asked the sailor.

"See if you can guess," said Ricardo. "Remember, we're 10 times as productive making hitechs and only 5 times as productive making lotechs."

"Then it must be our lotechs that will become more expensive than their lotechs, even while our hitechs are still cheaper than their hitechs," said the sailor.

"Exactly," Ricardo smiled.

"So," said the sailor, "we'll specialize in producing hitechs, consuming some and exporting the rest, while they'll specialize in producing lotechs, consuming some and exporting the rest."

"Now notice something," said Ricardo. "We could have predicted the free trade outcome by checking comparative advantage. We're 10 times as productive in hitechs but only 5 times as productive in lotechs, so we have a comparative advantage in hitechs and they have a comparative advantage in lotechs. Sure enough, if we open up free trade, prices will adjust so that we each specialize in producing and exporting the good in which we have a comparative advantage. And that makes both lands better off."

"But wait," said Autarkas. "The trade must be at a ratio between 1 to 2 and 1 to 4—for example, 1 hitech for 3 lotechs (10 hitechs for 30 lotechs)—to make both better off. You haven't shown that."

"You are difficult to satisfy, Autarkas. I like that. You'd make a good economist. Alas, that would indeed take a numerical example. But the example would show that when prices adjust under free trade, the ratio would in fact end up somewhere between 1 to 2 and 1 to 4, so both lands benefit."

"I have another objection," said Autarkas. "You assume prices will rise in Capital Land and fall in Labor Land until one good from each land becomes cheaper. But what if prices are slow to adjust? What then?"

"That's easy," replied Ricardo. "Suppose prices are absolutely fixed. Initially, everyone tries to buy our goods and no one tries to buy goods made in Labor Land. So at the banks, Labor Landers try to exchange labs for caps so they can buy our goods— they supply labs and demand caps—but no Capital Lander tries to exchange caps for labs. So at the banks, there is demand for caps but no supply of caps. Suppose the exchange rate was initially 1 lab for 1 cap. With caps in short supply but high demand, the banks will change the exchange rate. They may now require 2 labs for 1 cap. The cap *appreciates* and the lab *depreciates* in value—now 2 labs, not 1, are needed to get 1 cap."

"But now," said the sailor, "our goods are more expensive to Labor Landers. Even though the price in caps is fixed, the price in labs has doubled."

"Very good," said Ricardo.

"And Labor Land goods are cheaper to us," continued the sailor, "because even though the price in labs is fixed, the price in caps has halved."

"Exactly," said Ricardo. "So even if prices are fixed, a flexible exchange rate will make our goods more expensive to Labor Landers, and their goods cheaper to us. Eventually, one of the two goods will be more expensive when we make it and cheaper when they make it. So everyone will try to buy that good from Labor Land, not from us. Of course, that good will be a lotech. Now, at the banks, we will be supplying caps and demanding labs so we can buy their lotechs, and Labor Landers will still be supplying labs and demanding caps to buy our hitechs. At just the right exchange rate, the demand for caps will equal the supply of caps (and the demand for labs will equal the supply of labs) and the banks will have no reason to change the exchange rate."

"So," said the sailor, "once again they will specialize in lotechs and we will specialize in hitechs."

"That's right," said Ricardo. "So it doesn't matter whether prices rise and fall, or the exchange rate changes, or there is a combination of both—the result will be the same. Free trade will result in each land specializing in the good in which it has comparative advantage."

Fear of Trade

The sailors did not need to hear Ricardo to favor free trade. They were all for it because they would clearly profit from it. But people in Labor Land and Capital Land were another matter. Fear swept over Labor Land as soon as the ship from Capital Land left to return home.

"I've heard they're more productive in everything," said a frightened Labor Lander. "It is said they are 10 times as productive in making hitechs, and 5 times as productive in making lotechs. If we try to trade with them, they'll overpower us! We'll never be able to compete in anything, to sell anything. Free trade with Capital Land will be a disaster!"

Fortunately, when the second ship from Capital Land arrived in Labor Land, Ricardo was aboard. Immediately, he went directly to a TV studio where Labor Land's most popular talk show was in progress. As soon as Ricardo was introduced, the talk show host demanded that he explain why Labor Land wouldn't get slaughtered by trading with a productive powerhouse like Capital Land. The talk show audience was in a frenzy, and for a moment Ricardo was frightened.

"Don't worry," whispered the host. "The people we let in are always that way. It's good for our ratings. People love to watch hysterical people on TV."

"How interesting," whispered Ricardo to the host. "It's the same in Capital Land. The only difference is that the quality of our TV picture is much better than yours, so hysterical facial expressions can be seen more clearly by viewers. I suppose that's something you can look forward to under free trade."

Ignoring the shouting and frenzy, Ricardo calmly repeated the explanation he had given in Capital Land. "Suppose for a moment you can't sell anything because your prices are too high, and you want to buy everything from Capital Land because its prices are lower."

"Yeah!" screamed the audience. "Our factories will all shut down and we'll all be out of work!"

"Not at all," said Ricardo. "With everyone trying to buy goods made in Capital Land, its prices will rise. With no one trying to buy goods made in Labor Land, your prices will fall. This will all happen very quickly. Soon, one of your goods will be cheaper, and people in Capital Land will want to buy it. That good will be lotech, and you will specialize in its production, sell it to Capital Landers, and use your earnings to import hitechs. You'll do very well and be better off than you were before trade began. Now would you like me to explain how I know you will succeed at lotechs rather than hitechs?"

"No," said the talk show host, "that won't be necessary." No one in the audience was screaming anymore. In fact, half were yawning, and half had fallen asleep.

"But I've got a smashing numerical example," Ricardo said with enthusiasm.

The talk show host saw a frantic cut sign from the control

room. He led Ricardo by the hand off the stage. Later, he learned that his show's ratings had plunged drastically during the five minutes that Ricardo had been speaking. True, many TVs remained tuned to his station, but only because the viewers had fallen asleep.

Nevertheless, Ricardo offered to give more lectures and numerical examples, but the editorial in Labor Land's leading newspaper spoke for the nation: "We'll trade, we'll trade, but please go home, Mr. Ricardo!"

And so Ricardo returned home. Upon arriving in Capital Land, he found that a remarkable change had occurred. Initially, trade with Labor Land had been considered pointless. As Autarkas had said, "We're more productive in everything. Why trade?" Ricardo had persuaded Autarkas that Capital Land would benefit from trade with Labor Land, despite its absolute advantage in all goods. But now, to Ricardo's surprise, he found that fear of trade had spread among Capital Landers. He immediately went on a TV talk show to find out why.

"Our audience is very angry with you, Mr. Ricardo," whispered the host. "That's why we're having you on. Audience anger is great for our ratings."

"What seems to be the trouble?" Ricardo asked the audience.

"I'll tell you what the trouble is!" shouted one person. "You want us to trade with Labor Land. Well, we just found out that wages in Labor Land are much lower than the wages we are paid here in Capital Land. We'll never compete with them. Their costs are so low, they'll charge a lower price for everything. They'll make and sell everything, and we'll make and sell nothing."

"Yeah!" screamed the audience. "Our factories will all shut down and we'll all be out of work!"

"How ironic," Ricardo told the audience. "That's exactly what the Labor Landers said. But they predicted disaster from free trade because we're a productive powerhouse—more productive in making everything than they are. But now you are also predicting disaster from free trade because their wages and costs are much lower. Fortunately, your fear is as baseless as theirs."

"Why?" shouted the audience.

"Let me explain," said Ricardo calmly. "Suppose for a moment you can't sell anything because your wages, costs, and prices are higher, and you want to buy everything from Labor Land because its wages, costs, and prices are lower. With everyone trying to buy goods made in Labor Land, its wages, costs, and prices will rise. With no one trying to buy goods made in Capital Land, our wages, costs, and prices will fall. This will all happen very quickly. Soon, one of our goods will be cheaper, and people in Labor Land will want to buy it. That good will be hitech, and you will specialize in its production, sell it to Labor Landers, and use your earnings to import lotechs. You'll do very well and be better off than you were before trade began. Now, would you like me to explain how I know you will succeed at hitechs rather than lotechs?"

"No," said the talk show host, "that won't be necessary." No one in the audience was screaming anymore. In fact, half were yawning, and half had fallen asleep.

"But I've got a smashing numerical example," Ricardo said with enthusiasm.

The talk show host saw a frantic cut sign from the control room. He led Ricardo by the hand off the stage. Later, he learned that his show's ratings had plunged drastically during the five minutes that Ricardo had been speaking. True, many TVs remained tuned to his station, but only because the viewers had fallen asleep.

"Somehow I feel this has all happened before," said Ricardo wistfully.

Valid Concerns

"Ricardo, we'd like to have a word with you."

"Who are you four gentlemen?"

"We're Heckscher, Ohlin, Stolper, and Samuelson."

"What can I do for you?" asked Ricardo.

"Please don't misunderstand us," said Samuelson. "We have

the greatest admiration for your theory of comparative advantage and your demonstration that free trade benefits both lands even when one land is more productive in making every good. As economists, we find your reasoning and numerical examples to be as exciting as life on this earth ever gets."

"Thank you, kindred spirits," said Ricardo.

"However," said Samuelson, "there is one shortcoming from free trade that we economists should confess."

"Please explain," said Ricardo.

"It's important to recognize," said Heckscher and Ohlin in unison, "that each good in each land is made with two factors of production: labor and capital. We've been able to show that each country will successfully export the good that uses a lot of its abundant factor. So Capital Land will export hitechs because hitechs are produced with a lot of capital, and Labor Land will export lotechs because lotechs are produced with a lot of labor."

"Your analysis with two factors of production, labor and capital, is simply fascinating," cried Ricardo. "I used only labor in my analysis."

"We take it a step further," said Stolper and Samuelson in unison. "We can show that free trade helps a land's abundant factor and harms a land's scarce factor. In other words, free trade will raise the real wage of low-skilled workers in Labor Land where such labor is abundant, but will reduce the real wage of low-skilled workers in Capital Land where such labor is scarce. The reason is simple. Free trade causes Labor Land to expand production of lotechs, which uses a lot of low-skilled labor, so wages get bid up. But free trade causes Capital Land to shrink production of lotechs, so wages of low-skilled workers get forced down."

"But you do find that each land gains from free trade, don't you?" asked Ricardo.

"Yes, we do," replied Samuelson. "The gain to everyone else in Capital Land is much greater than the loss to low-skilled workers through the fall in their wages. To be precise, we show that if everyone who gains from trade compensated those who lose, then everyone in the land would be better off."

"Excellent," said Ricardo.

"However," said Samuelson, "we economists should surely advocate not only free trade, but compensation to those who lose from it."

"How should the compensation be implemented?" asked Ricardo.

"In two ways," replied Samuelson. "First, taxpayers should help finance the retraining of workers who lose jobs when free trade causes some industries to contract. And second, in Capital Land, we must explain that because free trade may well harm low-skilled workers, it is important to have a progressive tax system, an earned income credit, and social insurance to compensate these workers so that free trade will in fact benefit everyone."

Two citizens who had been listening now spoke up. "I have another concern," said Labortas. "Labor Land has much weaker labor standards than we do. For example, they permit child labor, poor working conditions, and very long work days. As a result, they outcompete us in goods involving such labor. Even worse, our industries lobby to weaken our labor standards, complaining that there should be a level playing field."

"Why, your concern is similar to mine," said Environmentas. "Labor Land has much weaker pollution standards than we do. As a result, they outcompete us in goods involving pollution. Even worse, our industries lobby to weaken our pollution standards, complaining that there should be a level playing field."

"You've both raised valid concerns," said Econo, one of the brightest young economists in Capital Land. "We economists must show some common sense. In our standard models, people get satisfaction only from consumption of goods. But our people actually care about whether production involves the exploitation of labor or the degradation of the environment. Once we recognize that these are legitimate preferences of our people, sensible economists should have an open mind about proposals to restrict trade when exploitation of labor or environmental degradation is severe."

"But we must be careful," warned Ricardo. "When a land

becomes open to free trade, the industries in which it has a comparative disadvantage are forced to contract by foreign competition. Most people in both lands benefit from trade, but naturally, workers and managers in the contracting industries are unhappy. They are likely to accuse the other land of extreme exploitation or pollution, whether valid or not, to get restrictions on trade and protect their position."

"Very true, Ricardo," said Econo. "We must use our common sense and strike a balance. Labor Land is less productive than we are, and therefore has a lower wage and a lower standard of living. Labor Landers may feel they can't afford to match our labor and environmental standards at this stage of their development. We should therefore not insist on such a matching in order to trade with Labor Land. At the same time, we should insist that Labor Land avoid extreme labor exploitation and environmental degradation before we are willing to trade." Econo's advice was followed. In the trade agreement signed by the governments of Labor Land and Capital Land, Labor Land agreed to improve its working conditions, reduce its work day, eliminate child labor, and reduce its pollution. Capital Land did not insist that wages, labor conditions, or environmental quality match its own. Capital Land enacted programs to help its low-skilled workers cope with the effects of trade.

And so, our tale of two islands comes to a happy end. Having overcome their baseless fears, and having responded to valid concerns, the two islands moved boldly forward, trading freely, and benefiting mutually.

8 THE SOCIAL CONTRACT

Once upon a time in a faraway land there lived a people in a state of nature. There were no laws to tell them what they couldn't do, no police to order them around, and no government to make them pay taxes. You might think it was heaven on earth. But, alas, it wasn't.

Each spring the Earnest family planted crops and each fall they harvested them. But each winter the Bully family ate most of the crops, while the Earnest family had barely enough crop to survive. How did this happen? Very simply. Each fall, just as the Earnests finished harvesting their crops, they were paid a visit by the Bully family.

"Here come the Bullies again!" cried the littlest Earnest, pointing out the window of their small cottage. In a few seconds the door flung open and in came the Bullies. They were big, they were mean, and there were plenty of them. "Where's the crop?" growled Big Bully himself. Trembling, the Earnests pointed to their modest barn. Soon every Bully was carrying the stored corn to the Bully wagon. In a half hour they had loaded up nearly all the crop. Suddenly the door was flung open again. It was Nasty Bully herself.

"Quit shaking and whimpering," she said with contempt. "We left you just enough to make it through the winter. After all, if you starved, who would slave for us next year?" Then she turned and cackled uproariously until she got to the huge Bully wagon. In a few seconds, the Bully wagon was gone, and so was most of the Earnest crop.

"It's not fair," cried the littlest Earnest.

"Can't we do something about it?" asked Mother Earnest.

"Not by ourselves," said Father Earnest. "The Bullies are too strong."

"But we can get help," said Mother Earnest. "We're not the only ones the Bullies pick on. They do the same thing to other families. They take tools from the Smiths, clothes from the Weavers, and a huge volume of products from the energetic Productives. They ignore the Lazies, who don't produce anything, but they take most of the meager output of the Tryers, who work long and hard but are able to produce very little."

"Let's call a secret meeting of all the families the Bullies prey on," said Father Earnest. "I think I know how we can solve our Bully problem."

Our Government

In the dead of night, while the Bullies slept soundly, the families walked silently through a moonlit field, traversed a dark woods, and finally emerged into a clearing. They lit a fire and sat near its warmth.

"I've called this meeting," began Father Earnest, "because our state of nature just isn't working. The Bullies take advantage of all of us. It's time we did something about it."

"What can we do?" whispered Timidas.

"We need to protect what we produce," replied Earnest. "I propose that each family contribute one member—a strong one—to a new organization. It will be called the *police*. Its mission will be to protect everyone from the Bullies."

"The police will need weapons," said Productive. "The Smiths make weapons. They can make them and give them to our police."

The members of the Fair family shifted uneasily. Finally Father Fair spoke up. "We don't think the whole burden should be put on the Smiths just because they make weapons. We should all share the burden."

Economas interjected, "That's easy enough. Let the Smiths make the weapons. Since every household, except the Lazies, earns coins selling what it produces, each household can contribute some coins to the police. The police will use some of the coins to buy weapons from the Smiths, and will use the rest of the coins to buy the food and clothes they need."

Suspicious spoke up. "But how do we make sure the police don't violate our rights while they track down Bullies?"

Politicas replied, "We need courts and judges to protect us from our own police, as well as to decide our disputes peacefully, and make sure only the guilty go to jail, while the innocent go free. We will need some taxes to pay the judges."

Next Mother Fair asked, "How do we make sure that everyone contributes coins, and how do we decide how much each household should contribute?"

Politicas replied, "We need to form a government. We must remember that it is *our* government, created by us, to do our bidding. It is up to us to decide what our government can and cannot do. Of course, it is impractical to have our government make decisions by calling meetings where every family participates. We're all too busy for that. Instead, we should vote to elect representatives who will meet regularly and make decisions. We know the first thing we want our representatives to do: hire and supervise the police, decide how much tax each household must pay, and make sure that every household pays its assigned tax. If they do a poor job, we'll replace them in the next election."

"Much as I hate to admit it," said Libertas, "we must give our government the power to do these things." Everyone nodded in agreement.

And so, within in a few days, the first election was held, a government formed, police chosen, and taxes collected. The next time the Bullies came to someone's house, they were shocked. Before they knew what had hit them, they were in handcuffs, riding in the new police wagon to the new jail.

Things were fine for a while, but one day the littlest Earnest climbed to the highest mountain peak in the land, looked out in the distance, squinted, and then climbed down the mountain as fast as he could and ran home shouting, "Foreign Bullies, foreign Bullies! I saw them, I saw them!"

"Tell us what you saw," said Mother Earnest, trying to calm him down.

"Far in the distance, I saw people with weapons, and horses, and big wagons. They looked just like our Bullies."

"Were they riding toward us?" asked Mother Earnest.

"Not yet," he replied. "But they could. And if they do, we'll be in big trouble."

Mother Earnest called a meeting that very night. And everyone agreed that the police could not handle an invasion by foreign Bullies. Moreover, they realized they were in great danger from foreign Bullies, because word might have spread that their own Bullies were no longer in control. Defensas said, "I propose we immediately create a *military*, far stronger than our police, to protect us against invasion by foreign Bullies."

"This will require a lot more taxes than we needed for the police," said Father Earnest.

"We have no choice," replied Defensas. "Our victory over our own Bullies will mean little if we are conquered by foreign Bullies."

And so it was agreed. Much higher taxes were raised, and a strong military was established. A message about the new military was sent to foreign lands.

A month later, the littlest Earnest climbed the same mountain and stared out in the distance in all directions. No matter how hard he looked, he saw no signs of anyone approaching with weapons, horses, and wagons. "They must have heard about our new military," he said with a proud smile.

The Free Market

Exactly one year later, the citizens met on a moonlit night in the very same clearing to celebrate the first anniversary of their new government and to assess its impact.

Productive spoke first. "Things are great. With the Bullies behind bars, my family has the skill and energy to invent and produce things people need, so this year we earned a huge volume of coins. All we want our government to do is to keep our own Bullies out of our way and prevent foreign Bullies from causing trouble."

Immediately Socialas stood up. "I couldn't disagree with you more, Productive. Now that we have formed a government, we should use it to its maximum potential. Today, every family makes its own decision about what and how much to produce. There is no central coordination and planning to make sure there is enough of good X but not too much of good Y. Every family pursues its own self-interest, trying to make as much profit as it can, without thinking about the needs of our whole society."

"What should we do?" asked Naivas.

"I propose," continued Socialas, "that the government coordinate and plan our economy. The government should draw up a detailed economic plan specifying how much of goods X, Y, and Z should be produced. Then the government should employ each family, and assign each one a specific productive task to make sure that the plan is carried out. If we don't do this, we'll have chaos."

An uneasiness came over the people. On the one hand, most cherished the freedom to decide on their own economic activity without government orders. But on the other hand, Socialas' point seemed plausible. Wouldn't there be chaos unless the government specified the required amounts of goods X, Y, and Z and employed every family to make sure the required amounts were produced?

At this very moment, the most brilliant member of the Smith family, Adam, rose to his feet. In his hand he held a lengthy

manuscript. "I rise to answer Socialas," Adam Smith said calmly.
"But have no fear," he soothed the crowd. "I will not attempt to
read this manuscript to you. I have just completed it after several
years of work. It's called *The Wealth of Nations,* and I hope that
some of you will find the time and interest to read it. Tonight, I
will briefly summarize it in order to answer Socialas."

The people looked at Adam Smith with anticipation. He was
not merely the most brilliant member of his family. Many felt he
was the most brilliant person in their entire society. Then Smith
began to speak.

"Each family is now free to decide what and how much to
produce, and with the Bullies removed, each knows that if it
produces more, it will consume more. Each is free to pursue its
own economic self-interest. You all appreciate that freedom. But
many of you worry that Socialas is right, that the result will be
chaos. I want to assure you, this evening, that your fears are
unfounded.

"By forming a government to protect us from the Bullies,"
Smith continued, "a remarkable system has come into being: the
free market. Socialas says that chaos will result, but let me begin
with this question: Has there been chaos this year?"

"Not really," said Earnest. "In fact, the economy has worked
very well. All the families, except the Lazies, have been working
hard to produce high-quality products at the lowest possible cost,
and consumers seem pleased."

"But," asked Smith, "why do producers care about high quality and low cost? Aren't they concerned mainly about their own
profit?"

"Yes," replied Earnest, "every producer strives to make a
profit. I must confess that our family cares about profit too."

"Yet you say consumers seem pleased. Now, how can this
be?" Smith asked with a twinkle in his eye.

"I'm not sure," replied Earnest.

"Let me ask you a question," said Smith. "How does your
family decide what and how much to produce in order to make a
profit?"

"Well," said Earnest, "first we think about what we're best at making. We're best at growing crops. We know we shouldn't try to make clothes or tools. The Weavers are much better at making clothes, and the Smith family—except for you, Adam—is much better at making tools."

"Yes," said Adam, "I have disappointed my family by teaching and writing instead of making tools. They are particularly upset about the subject I have chosen: economics. They say I have disgraced them by becoming an economist. But I'm hopeful that my book, *The Wealth of Nations,* will prove to be a different kind of powerful tool, worthy of a Smith. History will judge. But let's get back to your family, Earnest. How do you decide which crops will be the most profitable?"

"We see that consumers like corn better than stinkus. If we grow corn, we make a profit. If we grow stinkus, we don't."

"And why do you work hard to produce your crop at lowest possible cost?" asked Smith.

"Because we have to charge a price that covers our cost. A low cost lets us charge a low price."

"I suspect," interjected Socialas, "that you want to charge a high price even if your cost is low, so you can make a huge profit."

"I confess," said Earnest, "that you're right about what we want. But we can't do it."

"Why not?" asked Socialas. "Does your conscience stop you?"

"No, its not our conscience," replied Earnest. "It's our competition."

"I don't follow," said Socialas.

"Well," said Earnest, "we're not the only family growing corn. A dozen families grow corn. If we charge a price much above cost, they'll offer consumers a lower price, and no one will buy corn from us."

"I suspect," interjected Socialas, "that you want to grow low-quality corn because it's cheaper."

"Once again," said Earnest, "I confess that you're right about what we want, but we can't do it, not because of our conscience, but because of our competition. Most consumers are willing to pay a higher price for high-quality corn. We actually make more profit producing high-quality corn, even though the higher cost makes us charge a higher price."

"And so," said Adam Smith, "you make a profit by figuring out what consumers want, and producing it for them. Competition prevents you from over-charging and compels you to produce a high quality with the lowest possible cost."

"That's true," said Earnest.

"But," said Socialas, "he admits that his family and all the others are pursuing their own self-interest. No one is making sure that their decisions serve the public interest."

"Socialas," replied Adam Smith with a smile, "they are indeed freely pursuing their own interest, and no earthly government is telling them what or how much to produce. But in a free market they are led by an *Invisible Hand* to make decisions and pursue economic activities that serve the public interest."

The people nodded their agreement with Adam Smith, and Socialas sat down, dejected.

Social Insurance

As Socialas sat down, Father Fair stood up to speak. "Adam Smith has brilliantly shown us the virtues of a free market. Except Socialas, we are all convinced that our government should not employ families to make goods X, Y, and Z, or interfere with each family's decisions about what and how much to produce. But though we have rejected Socialas' radical role for the government, we must still ask whether there is a more limited role our government should perform as a complement to the free market."

Productive replied, "All we want our government to do is to keep our own Bullies out of our way and prevent foreign Bullies from causing trouble."

Father Fair replied, "I believe there is something else we should instruct our government to do. It's great that the Bullies are behind bars and that the Productives can produce as much as they can without fear it will be stolen. We all benefit from their skill and energy. But not everyone has as much skill and energy as the Productives. I'm not concerned about the Lazies—at least not the grown-ups. They simply don't want to work, they earn nothing, and it's certainly fair that they consume very little, surviving on the few coins they receive from Charitas.

"But," continued Father Fair, "I *am* concerned about the Tryers. They work as long and as hard as the Productives, but they produce so much less. No matter how hard they try, they barely earn enough to survive. They need supervision, so they work for the Productives, who assign them tasks and pay them according to what they produce. You can't blame the Productives for paying them a low wage because the Tryers produce a small amount, but the low wage means they can't afford to save anything. You can't blame the Productives for laying them off when sales are slow. And when Tryers get too old to work, or need costly medical care, they're in trouble. Only the generosity of Charitas keeps the Tryers from starving when they're unemployed or too old to work, and gets them essential medical care. But Charitas is getting old, and soon there may be no one around to help the Tryers."

"That's the way it goes," replied Marketas. "The only proper role of government is to take care of the Bullies so that the free market can work. Then everyone is free to produce whatever he can and keep whatever he earns. The only thing government should do is raise enough taxes to pay the police and the military to protect everyone from Bullies and protect everyone's earnings from theft."

"But we can do better," said Father Fair. "We all agree that a state of nature is unfair, that it rewards the Bullies and harms everyone else. So we agree that we needed to create a government, and that our government should levy taxes, pay the police and military, and unleash a free market. And we agree that we should instruct our government to let the Productives earn and consume more than any other family because they produce more and we all benefit from their skill and energy. But why shouldn't we also instruct our government to help people like the Tryers?"

"The free market is natural," answered Marketas, "and the outcomes of a free market should therefore be accepted as natural. I'm opposed to our government tampering with the natural outcomes of a free market. Such tampering is unfair and unnatural."

"But," replied Father Fair, "while the free market is wonderfully productive, it is not natural. In the state of nature there was no free market. The Productives suffered along with everyone else. It was the Bullies who triumphed in the state of nature. We needed to invent our government in order to create a free market. But once we recognize that the free market is not natural and depends on our government, it makes sense to ask whether we should instruct our government to do anything else. Shouldn't we use our government to help the Tryers as well as helping the Productives?"

Marketas shook his head. "The only way to make the Tryers better off is to make the Productives worse off. You could instruct our government to take so many coins from the Productives and give so many coins to the Tryers that they would consume equally. But not only is that unfair—after all, we all benefit more from the Productives than the Tryers—but it would destroy the incentive of people to become as productive as they can be. Why make the effort to develop skill if you will not be allowed to consume the fruits of your higher skill? And if potentially productive people don't develop their skill, we will all miss the products they could have invented but didn't."

"I agree, Marketas," replied Father Fair. "If we instructed our government to tax the Productives so much and give so much to the Tryers that they both consumed equally, the outcome would be both unfair and disastrous. Neither the Productives nor the Tryers would work at all. But I'm proposing something much less extreme."

"Tell us," said Earnest.

"We should instruct our government," replied Father Fair, "to set up three social insurance programs: unemployment insurance, Social Security, and health insurance. The first would pay benefits to the unemployed; the second, to the old; and the third, to the sick. Our government would raise the coins it needs for social insurance by taxation."

"You better not be too generous with these social insurance benefits," warned Incentivas. "If you give an unemployed person a benefit as high as her former wage, she won't try to get another job. If you give an old person a benefit as high as her former wage, she won't save anything when she's working age, and our banks won't have the funds to lend businesses to use to make investments in technology from which we all benefit. And if you pay the entire medical bill of a sick person, she will have no incentive to consider cost when she orders medical care and we will all pay inflated taxes to cover her inflated medical costs."

"Your warnings are wise, Incentivas," replied Father Fair. "We must strike a balance. The unemployed person must get a benefit that is only a percentage of her former wage, so she can survive but still has a strong incentive to find another job as quickly as possible. The old person must get a benefit that is only a percentage of her former wage, so she can survive but still has a strong incentive to do some saving when she is working age. And the sick person must get a benefit that is only a percentage of her medical bill, so she can afford medical care she needs but still has an incentive to weigh the cost of anything she orders."

"Would these percentages be the same for everyone?" asked Earnest.

"I think it would be better," replied Father Fair, "to vary the percentages. Low earners like the Tryers should be given a high percentage, because despite their effort, their wage is low and they can hardly afford to save anything. Low earners like the Tryers might receive a benefit for unemployment or old age that is 60 percent of their former low wage, and a benefit that is 95 percent of their medical bill; high earners like the Productives might receive a benefit for unemployment or old age that is 20 percent of their former high wage, and a benefit that is 75 percent of their medical bill. In other words, I favor a *progressive* benefit schedule for social insurance programs—the lower the earnings, the higher the percentage."

"I have one problem with your medical percentage," said Earnest. "Some unfortunate people incur enormous medical bills. The low earner may not be able to afford to pay even 5 percent of the whole bill, and even the high earner may be unable to afford paying 25 percent of the whole bill."

"You're right," replied Father Fair. "Under my medical benefit schedule, once a household has paid an amount equal to a certain percentage of its income, it would not have to pay any more that year."

"Would this percentage of income be the same for everyone?" asked Earnest.

"Once again," said Father Fair, "I think it would be better to vary the percentage. For example, it might be 1 percent of income for the Tryers, but 5 percent of income for the Productives."

"But why should we instruct our government to provide insurance?" asked Marketas. "Insuras and her family do a nice job of selling private insurance under our free market. Why can't we rely on private insurance for unemployment, old age, and medical care?"

Economas turned and faced Marketas. "My dear Marketas, you know I teach the virtues of relying on the free market for almost everything we make. I argue vigorously against Socialas who wants our government to employ everyone and make everything. We need a free market with competition, not a government monopoly, to have a productive economy. But our beloved free market does a poor job with certain kinds of insurance. Tell me, what kind of insurance does Insuras sell?"

"Mainly wagon and home insurance," answered Marketas. "With wagon insurance, you're covered if your wagon injures someone and you owe huge damages. With home insurance, you're covered if a fire destroys your home."

"Yes," said Economas, "Insuras does a nice job with wagon and home insurance. But does Insuras sell unemployment insurance?"

"Come to think of it," answered Marketas, "she doesn't."

"No, she doesn't," said Economas. "And do you know why not?"

"No," answered Marketas, puzzled.

"Because," continued Economas, "she would be glad to sell unemployment insurance to the Productives even at a low price, because they'll probably never become unemployed. But the Productives won't buy insurance, because they can handle a brief unemployment spell with their own saving. On the other hand, Insuras won't sell insurance to the Lazies, who would immediately start collecting forever. She might like to sell to people like the Tryers, but she can't always tell whether a person will act like a Tryer or a Lazy. If a person wants to buy insurance, there's a good chance he'll act like a Lazy. So Insuras would have to set a high price. But then the Tryers won't think it's a good deal, only the Lazies will buy it, and Insuras will have to raise the price even further. Eventually, even the Lazies will think it's a bad deal. That's why Insuras doesn't sell unemployment insurance. We need our government to provide it."

"But," replied Marketas, "Insuras does sell old age insurance (which requires contributions while the person works and during retirement pays benefits for as long as the person lives), and medical insurance."

"Unfortunately, Marketas, there are several problems," replied Economas. "Let me begin with old age insurance. People like the Tryers simply don't earn a high enough wage to be able to afford to save enough for retirement. They need most of what the Productives pay them to subsist while they're working. So they can't afford to save enough or to buy old age insurance from Insuras.

"Then there are families like the Unluckies," continued Economas. "They save while they work, but misfortune strikes. A few years before retirement they happen to lose their jobs through no fault of their own, and they're forced to use up their savings until they find another job. Or they put their savings into stocks of companies that unexpectedly have difficulty selling their products, so the value of their stock plummets.

"Finally there are the Myopics, who earn a high enough wage, but they just don't think about what will happen when they get old. They spend all their coins today, and when they get old, they find themselves in trouble. Perhaps they deserve to starve in old age, but many of us (especially Charitas) won't let them—after all, they do work hard up until retirement. So we end up bailing them out with our coins, and they get away without saving."

Mother Fair interjected, "Rather than the rest of us bearing their burden, it would be fairer to make the Myopics contribute coins while they're working rather than letting them get a free ride. Only our government can make them bear their fair share of the burden by taxing them while they work."

"So," concluded Economas, "while some families save successfully on their own or buy enough old age insurance from Insuras, many do not. It makes sense to instruct our government to provide old age insurance so that everyone who worked when they were younger lives decently in retirement. Everyone would earn old age protection by paying taxes during their work life. If a family wants to live better than that, it must save on its own."

"Would the taxes of workers go straight out to retirees, or instead be invested in stocks and bonds to be used when workers retire?" asked Incentivas.

"That's a good question," replied Economas. "We should discuss the pros and cons of each method at a future meeting. Here I want to argue only that our government should provide old age insurance financed by our taxes."

"What about medical insurance?" asked Marketas.

"Yes," replied Economas, "some families buy medical insurance from Insuras. But, again, the Tryers can't afford it. And some families, like the Unhealthies, are not offered insurance at an affordable price. One of the Unhealthies has a chronic costly medical problem. You can't blame Insuras for refusing to offer insurance to the Unhealthies, because Insuras would lose a lot of money enrolling such costly families."

"Any family," said Mother Fair, "could suddenly come down with a chronic, costly medical problem. Would that family lose its insurance?"

"Not immediately," replied Economas. "But Insuras purposely

limits the insurance contract to one year. You can't blame Insuras for refusing to renew the insurance as soon as the year is up."

"True, I can't blame Insuras," said Mother Fair, "but I find this situation very disturbing. Any family can lose insurance just when it needs it most."

"But," interjected Marketas, "the situation is not as bad as that. Insuras often sells insurance to an employer, and agrees to cover and automatically renew all employees, whatever their medical costs. It's worth it to Insuras because it is profitable to enroll a large number of families all at once."

"You are quite right, Marketas," continued Economas. "As long as you can keep your job in a large business, your family is safe. But if you leave that workplace because you're too sick or too old, or become self-employed, employed by a small business, or unemployed, you're in trouble. Insuras will either charge you a very high price or refuse to sell you insurance."

"That could happen to any of us," said Mother Fair. "It will definitely happen once we get too old to work."

"So," concluded Economas, "while some families successfully obtain renewable medical insurance as long as they work for a large business, many do not. And even these families worry that they may lose this employment and medical insurance. It makes sense to instruct our government to provide medical insurance so that every family, lucky or unlucky, knows it will always be able to obtain needed medical care. Remember, every patient would be required to pay a percentage of her own medical bill until the burden becomes too great in a single year. Our government should provide universal, fair medical insurance, not free medical care."

The Social Insurance State

"What about the Lazies?" asked Earnest. "They're able to work but they just don't."

"I think we should help them too," said Compassionas. "They have a need for food, clothing, and shelter, just like the rest of us.

My motto is, 'To each according to his need.' So I think we need a fourth program, 'welfare,' to give coins to the Lazies."

Mother Fair responded, "True, the Lazies have a need, but they also have a responsibility. If we all refused to work, we would all starve, including the Lazies. It would be unfair to give coins to the Lazies when the Tryers work so hard to earn enough coins to survive. Welfare should give coins only to people genuinely unable to work due to physical or mental incapacity."

"I agree about the Lazies," replied Earnest. "But there are some people who want to work, but they have low skill, and have trouble finding an employer who finds it profitable to hire them even at a subsistence wage."

"The Lazies say they want to work, but they just can't find a job," said Naivas.

"There is only one way to put someone to the test," said Economas. "Our government should provide last-resort low-wage jobs, not welfare, for anyone physically and mentally able to work. If someone can't find a job with a regular employer, that person should be given a last-resort low-wage job."

"But what jobs can the government offer these low-skilled people?" asked Earnest.

"There's plenty of low-skilled work that needs to be done," replied Economas. "Our parks and streets need constant cleaning. The walls of our buildings need graffiti removed."

"But can the government efficiently operate a jobs program?" asked Earnest.

"It might be better," said Economas, "to have the government contract with private firms to run the work projects. But the government must pay for the projects and make sure that enough are available so that anyone who wants to work gets the chance."

"Why must the jobs have a low wage?" asked Naivas.

"Because this work doesn't deserve a wage as high as the Tryers earn from a private employer," said Mother Fair.

"Moreover," added Economas, "we want everyone to have an incentive to prefer regular jobs to these last-resort jobs."

"But how can they survive on such a low wage?" asked Naivas. "Even the Tryers can barely survive."

"Our government should give a supplement to all low-wage workers," answered Economas, "whether the person works for a regular employer or in the last-resort jobs program. The supplement wouldn't be welfare because no one would get it unless they worked and earned a low wage; up to a point, the more they earned, the more supplement they would get. We can efficiently administer this supplement through our tax system, so I propose that we call the supplement the Earned Income Tax Credit. I'll explain the details at a future meeting."

"So," Earnest said, "our message will be this: There's no welfare if you can work but don't. But there's always a place to earn enough to survive: the last-resort jobs program. Though the wage is low, if you work hard, your supervisor will give you a letter of recommendation to help you get a higher-paying job with a regular employer."

"But what if someone gets the last-resort job," said Tryer, "but then makes little effort to do the job right?"

"Then that person must be fired," said Mother Fair, "and be given another chance a month or two later. A month or two without coins might change the attitudes of those who shirk the first time."

"But what about their children?" objected Compassionas. "Should children suffer because their parents won't work?"

"You ask a tough question," replied Mother Fair. "Remember, the children will be covered by our medical insurance program, because that will be universal and automatic. But they will still suffer if their parents refuse to work."

"We can't let lazy people extort coins from us by threatening to let their children starve," said Tryer.

"I agree," said Mother Fair. "Perhaps the best solution is to treat repeated shirkers as being guilty of child neglect. We already remove children from parents who severely neglect or abuse them. Refusing to take a job that can give your child food is surely severe neglect. Of course, this must be handled carefully, with due process and sensitivity. Clear warnings must be given. No child should be taken from a parent unless the child is in genuine danger. And a parent must be able to get the child back by working responsibly."

"So our social insurance programs would not make us a 'welfare state,' " said Earnest. "There would be welfare only for those physically or mentally unable to work. Everyone else would have to work to earn coins. Perhaps we should call ours a *social insurance state.*"

"I agree," said Mother Fair.

Educas spoke up. "I very much support our social insurance programs and jobs program. But we need one thing more. Education helps make an economy productive, but just as important, it is the key to a child's opportunity. Up until now, our schools have been private, and parents have had to pay the entire tuition themselves. But some families earn enough coins to pay the tuition of a high-quality school, while others earn barely enough to pay the low tuition of a low-quality school.

"This is wrong," said Mother Fair. "We should reduce the quality gap among our schools."

"The solution," said Educas, "is to levy taxes to pay for schools. The tax each family is assigned should vary with its consumption. Tax finance will enable children of all families to attend schools with decent quality."

"This doesn't mean," noted Economas, "that the government must use all tax revenue to finance free public schools. Some of the revenue should be used for scholarships for non-affluent families, so they have the ability to switch to a private school if they are very dissatisfied with their public school. That's a subject for a future meeting."

A Progressive Tax

"I propose," said Father Fair, "that the government use a *progressive* tax to raise the coins to pay for the military, the police, the judges, the schools, and the last-resort jobs program. It's all right for the social insurance programs to be financed mainly by an earmarked wage (payroll) tax so that each working person knows he has contributed and has earned insurance benefits through work. But for all other government expenditures, we should use a progressive tax."

"What's a progressive tax?" asked Earnest.

"It's a tax that takes a higher percentage from the affluent than from the non-affluent," answered Father Fair. "Economas, would you give us an example?"

"Certainly," replied Economas. "To keep it simple, let's assume there is only one Productive and one Tryer. Productive earns 100,000 coins this year, while Tryer, working just as long and hard, manages to earn only 10,000 coins, so the ratio of before-tax incomes is 10 (100,000/10,000). A proportional tax would take the same percentage from everyone; for example, a 20 percent proportional tax would raise 20,000 coins from Productive and 2,000 from Tryer, for a total tax revenue of 22,000. Productive would pay 10 times as much tax as Tryer, and Productive would have 80,000 coins left, while Tryer would have 8,000 left. Note that with a proportional tax, the ratio of after-tax incomes is 10 (80,000/8,000), the same as the ratio of before-tax incomes."

"How would the progressive tax be different?" asked Naivas.

"Under a progressive tax," said Economas, "Productive would pay a higher percentage than Tryer. For example, instead of both paying 20 percent, suppose Tryer pays 12 percent while Productive pays 20.8 percent. Then Tryer would pay 1,200 coins (.12 × 10,000) and Productive would pay 20,800 coins (.208 × 100,000), again for a total tax revenue of 22,000."

"Is that fair to Productive?" asked Arithmetas. "I just calculated that Productive would pay 17.3 times as much tax as Tryer (20,800/1,200 = 17.3), even though Productive earns 10 times as much income as Tryer."

"But," said Economas, "can you tell us, Arithmetas, how many times more would Productive be able to consume than Tryer?"

"That's easy enough," answered Arithmetas. "Productive will have 79,200 coins left after tax, while Tryer will have 8,800 coins left, so Productive will be able to consume 9 times as much as Tryer (79,200/8,800 = 9). That's remarkable. Even though the progressive tax makes Productive pay 17.3 times as much tax as Tryer, it still lets Productive consume 9 times as much as Tryer. That's not much less than the earnings ratio of 10."

"But," warned Marketas, "that drop from 10 to 9 may weaken the incentive of Productive to work his hardest."

"I would still work my hardest if I could consume 9 times as much," said Naivas.

"I admit," confessed Productive, "that I would still work my hardest. But you're missing the point. I earned 100,000 coins in the free market. Government has no right to take coins from me. The coins are my property. I'm entitled to consume 10 times as much as Tryer because I produced and earned 10 times as much."

"Aren't you overlooking one thing, Productive?" said Father Fair. "Without a government, taxes, and police, you would consume the same amount as Tryer, thanks to the Bullies—barely enough to avoid starvation. So if the government enacts a progressive tax where you pay 20.8 percent and Tryer 12 percent, you would consume 9 times more than Tryer. While 9 times under the progressive tax is not quite as good as 10 times under the proportional tax, it is still much better than the state of nature, where your consumption would be the same as his."

"I'd take 9 times," said Naivas.

"But it's still not fair," insisted Productive. "I produce 10 times as much, not 9 times as much."

"Yes," replied Father Fair, "you are blessed with the potential to develop high skill, and you work hard to develop it. We all benefit more from you than we do from Tryer, so I agree that you deserve to consume more than Tryer. But 9 times is certainly a lot more, even if it is less than 10."

"I think the Tryers deserve to consume as much as the Productives," said Egalitas. "Without government, they would consume the same, thanks to the Bullies. The Tryers work as long and as hard as the Productives. It's not their fault that they weren't given the potential to develop high skill. I say the government should tax the Productives more, and transfer coins to the Tryers rather than tax them, so that each Tryer ends up with the same coins as each Productive."

"Egalitas, I disagree with you for two reasons," replied Father Fair. "First, I don't think effort is all that matters for fairness. True, the Tryers give the same effort as the Productives. But the fact is that the rest of us benefit more from the Productives than we do from the Tryers. So I think it is fair to weigh actual productivity as well as effort. Second, your proposal is impractical. It would destroy the incentive of everyone to work hard, and we would all lose. Each Productive will work just as hard if each gets to consume 9 times, instead of 10 times, as much as each Tryer. But if we make the tax-transfer system much too progressive—if we go to your extreme of making everyone end up with equal consumption—then we will end up with poverty for everyone because no one will work hard."

A Progressive Income Tax or a Progressive Consumption Tax?

"I'm persuaded that our tax should be progressive," said Earnest. "But that still leaves open this question: Should the progressive rates apply to each family's income or to its consumption?"

"Good question," said Economas. "Which one we choose could have an important effect on our future standard of living. If families are taxed on their consumption, not their income, there will almost surely be more saving in our economy. This saving is put into banks that lend it to our business firms so they can invest in new machinery and technology. Saving is necessary to finance investment, and investment is what makes our productivity and standard of living rise."

"But is it fair to tax each family according to its consumption, rather than its income, even at progressive rates?" asked Mother Fair. "After all, consider the thrifty person who earns a high income but consumes little. He has a high ability to pay. Shouldn't he pay tax according to his ability?"

"Some are surely persuaded by this ability-to-pay argument," replied Father Fair. "But there is another way of looking at it. When a thrifty person takes only a small amount out of the economic pie to consume for his own enjoyment, he leaves more resources for others to consume, or for businesses to invest. That investment raises the future productivity, wages, and standard of living of everyone. True, he may get pleasure from saving, while others get pleasure from consuming. But the consequence for the rest of us is very different. The more someone saves, the higher is everyone else's future standard of living."

"So," said Mother Fair, "you believe that consequences are relevant to fairness, and therefore it is fairer to tax families according to what they take out of the pie for their own consumption."

"Yes," replied Father Fair.

"In that case," said Earnest, "it doesn't make sense to tax people when they transfer wealth through gifts or bequests, or when they inherit wealth."

"I agree," replied Father Fair. "Giving or receiving wealth does not remove resources from the economic pie. It does not reduce the resources available for businesses to invest. Only when someone consumes his wealth should he be taxed, and then at progressive rates."

"Not having wealth transfer taxes would surely be simpler," said Earnest. "But is it practical for each household to compute its annual consumption?"

"It is," replied Economas. "Each year a household must add its cash inflows, like wages and withdrawals from bank accounts, and subtract non-consumption cash outflows, such as deposits in saving or investment accounts, or purchases of stocks and bonds. What's left is the household's consumption. Of course, it's more complicated than this. (A tax return under the personal consumption tax is given in the appendix to chapter 3.) Some things are more complicated under a consumption tax, but others are more complicated under an income tax. I propose we devote a future meeting to these practical aspects. What is certain is that our future standard of living will be higher if we use a progressive consumption tax instead of a progressive income tax."

"And though some disagree," said Father Fair, "in my view our tax will be fairer if we choose a progressive consumption tax over a progressive income tax."

"Where can I learn more about the progressive personal consumption tax?" asked Earnest.

"In chapter 3 of this book and in a fine book by Laurence Seidman entitled *The USA Tax: A Progressive Consumption Tax* (1997)."

Our Constitution

At the next annual meeting to review the progress of their government, Politicas spoke first. "We should be proud of ourselves. We saw that the state of nature wasn't working, so we came together to form our government. We immediately agreed on the need for taxes to pay our police and judges, and soon after agreed on even higher taxes to pay our military. Socialas made the radical proposal that our government employ everyone and run our economy, but Adam Smith showed brilliantly why we should let the free market guide our economy instead. After Smith spoke, no one except Socialas wanted our government to employ everyone to make all goods and services. Some of us wanted to limit our government to the police, courts, and military. But the majority wanted our government to use taxes to finance several social insurance programs, a last-resort jobs program, welfare only for people genuinely unable to work, and elementary and secondary education. The majority opted for a progressive consumption tax to finance all government expenditures except the social insurance programs, which would be financed by a payroll tax.

"Instead of remaining in a state of nature," continued Politicas, "we entered into a social contract, specifying what our government would and would not do. Now that we have experimented, I propose that we embody our social contract in a written constitution. This will prevent disputes in the future about what our government can and cannot do, and ensure our rights and liberties. We must be humble enough to allow a procedure for amending the constitution. But amending it should be hard, not easy, so that it will occur only when a large majority concur."

Politicas was nominated to head a committee to draft a written constitution embodying the social contract. On the day the constitution was ratified by the people, the state of nature was declared gone forever, permanently replaced by a social contract utilizing a government created by the people for their benefit and guided by a written constitution. It was a day of celebration.

APPENDIX

U.S. Taxes: An International Perspective

Implementing all components of this social contract in the United States would require some increase in the ratio of taxes to GDP (gross domestic product). Table 8.1 shows that the United States is a very low-tax country by international standards. In the table, federal, state, and local taxes are included in "taxes"; federal taxes are about two-thirds of U.S. total taxes (non-tax revenues such as fees are excluded; if these were included, the U.S. ratio would be about 34 percent, while Denmark's ratio would be about 60 percent). Implementing all components of this social contract might raise the U.S. ratio to roughly 35 percent.

The Distribution of Income and Federal Taxes in the United States

Table 8.2 shows that in 1990 the richest 10 percent received 36.1 percent of the nation's pre-tax income; the richest 5 percent, 25.7 percent; and the richest 1 percent, 12.8 percent. What income

Table 8.1

Total Tax Revenue as Percentage of Gross Domestic Product (1994)

Denmark	51.6	Germany	39.3
Sweden	51.0	Ireland	37.5
Czech Rep.	47.3	New Zealand	37.0
Finland	47.3	Canada	36.1
Belgium	46.6	Spain	35.8
Netherlands	45.9	United Kingdom	34.1
Luxembourg	45.0	Switzerland	33.9
France	44.1	Portugal	33.0
Poland	43.2	Iceland	30.9
Austria	42.8	Australia	29.9
Greece	42.5	Japan	27.8
Italy	41.7	**United States**	**27.6**
Norway	41.2	Turkey	22.2
Hungary	41.0	Mexico	18.8

Unweighted Average:	
OECD Total	38.4
OECD America	27.5
OECD Pacific	31.6
OECD Europe	40.8
European Union	42.5

Source: Organization for Economic Cooperation and Development, *Revenue Statistics of OECD Member Countries 1965–1995* (Paris, 1996), Table 1, p. 74.

Table 8.2

Shares of Pre-tax Income for Affluent Families (%)

Families	1980	1985	1990	Income threshold in 1996
Top 10 percent	31.7	35.0	36.1	$108,704
Top 5 percent	21.4	24.5	25.7	$145,412
Top 1 percent	9.4	11.8	12.8	$349,438

Sources: 1993 Green Book (Committee on Ways and Means, U.S. House of Representatives, which cites source as Congressional Budget Office [CBO]), Table 17, p. 1506 for three left columns; U.S. Treasury, article in *Tax Notes* 70, no. 4 (January 22, 1996), p. 455 for right column.

Table 8.3

Total Federal Effective Tax Rates for Affluent Families (%)

Families	1980	1985	1990	1994a	1994b
Top 10 percent	28.7	24.4	26.0	27.0	29.2
Top 5 percent	29.7	24.4	26.2	27.4	30.4
Top 1 percent	31.9	24.5	26.3	28.0	33.2

Sources: 1993 Green Book (Committee on Ways and Means, U.S. House of Representatives, which cites source as CBO), Table 11, p. 1497 for three left columns; Congressional Budget Office memo, *OBRA-93* (1994), p. 32 for two right columns; 1994a is projection before 1993 tax act (OBRA-1993), 1994b is projection after 1993 tax act.

levels did it take to make it to each pre-tax income class? To make the numbers more meaningful for citizens in the mid-1990s, a projection for 1996 is given. To be in the richest 10 percent in 1996 requires an income of at least $108,704; in the richest 5 percent, $145,412; in the richest 1 percent, $349,438. The pre-tax income shares of the affluent increased during the 1980s. From 1980 to 1990, the share of the top 10 percent rose from 31.7 percent to 36.1 percent; the top 5 percent, from 21.4 percent to 25.7 percent; and the top 1 percent, from 9.4 percent to 12.8 percent.

Table 8.3 shows the effective (average) tax rate (the ratio of federal taxes to income). The tax rate includes all federal taxes. Of course, the highest tax rate an affluent household pays on its last $100 of income—its "marginal tax rate"—exceeds its effective tax rate because it pays lower rates on most of its income. Thus, a high-income person in 1985 was in a 50 percent tax bracket for labor income, interest, and dividends (though not capital gains)—the last $100 earned was taxed at 50 percent—but for the top 1 percent, the ratio of total tax to total income was just under 25 percent. Note that the 1993 tax act raised the tax rate of the affluent several points, but still left the richest 1 percent with an effective tax rate of 33.2 percent.

The headline for Table 8.4 is this: "The Affluent Pay a Large

Table 8.4

Shares of Total Federal Taxes Paid by Affluent Families (%)

Families	1980	1985	1990	1994a
Top 10 percent	39.1	39.2	41.6	42.7
Top 5 percent	27.4	27.5	29.8	31.0
Top 1 percent	12.8	13.3	14.9	15.8

Source: 1993 Green Book (Committee on Ways and Means, U.S. House of Representatives, which cites source as CBO), Table 25, p. 1515. 1994a is projection before 1993 tax act (OBRA-1993).

Table 8.5

Shares of After-tax Income for Affluent Families (%)

Families	1980	1985	1990
Top 10 percent	29.5	33.8	34.5
Top 5 percent	19.6	23.7	24.5
Top 1 percent	8.3	11.3	12.2

Source: 1993 Green Book (Committee on Ways and Means, U.S. House of Representatives, which cites source as CBO), Table 18, p. 1507.

Share of Federal Taxes." Despite the services of tax lawyers and accountants, most of the affluent pay substantial federal taxes. In 1990, the richest 10 percent paid 41.6 percent of federal taxes; the richest 5 percent, 29.8 percent, and the richest 1 percent, 14.9 percent. Since the payroll tax is proportional up to the $61,200 ceiling (1995) and regressive beyond, the primary cause of these large affluent tax shares is the progressive (graduated) rate schedule of the household income tax.

These tax shares may seem so large that it provokes the question: Is the affluent share of after-tax income much lower than its share of before-tax income? Table 8.5 shows that the answer is no. After the graduated income tax has done its work, their share is almost as great. The share of 1990 after-tax income is 34.5 percent for the top 10 percent (compared with 36.1 percent of pre-tax income in Table 8.2); 24.5 percent for the top 5 percent

Table 8.6

How to Compute Your Tax Under the 1995 Progressive Income Tax Schedule

If you are a family of four, you get four personal exemptions ($2,500 each), for a total of $10,000, and either a standard deduction of $6,550 or a set of itemized deductions. Assume you take the standard deduction. Then your first $16,550 of income is not taxable. Your taxable income is taxed at the following rates:

Taxable Income	Bracket Tax Rate (%)
$0–$39,000	15.0
$39,000–$94,000	28.0
$94,000–$144,000	31.0
$144,000–$257,000	36.0
$257,000 and over	39.6

If your *taxable* income is $357,000, what is the total tax that you must pay? You need to add five numbers:

$$.15 \times \$\ 39,000 = \$\ 5,850$$
$$.28 \times \$\ 55,000 = \$15,400$$
$$.31 \times \$\ 50,000 = \$15,500$$
$$.36 \times \$113,000 = \$40,680$$
$$.396 \times \$100,000 = \$39,600$$

TOTAL TAX = $117,030

Your total tax as a percent of your taxable income is 32.8% (117,030/357,000).

(vs. 25.7 percent of pre-tax income); and 12.2 percent for the top 1 percent (vs. 12.8 percent of pre-tax income). While the 1993 tax act probably reduced affluent after-tax income shares a little further, this headline for Table 8.5 still stands: "The Affluent Survive the Income Tax."

9 FUNDED SOCIAL SECURITY

I don't want to cause you any unnecessary anxiety, but I must tell you that the U.S. Social Security system faces a little problem in the future. Don't worry, I have a proposal to fix it. If implemented, my proposal will help solve that problem at the same time that it immediately raises our national saving rate.

Before I begin, let's take care of this question: "Don't we already have a giant Social Security fund?" The mistake is natural. After all, every properly managed private pension does have a big fund. And the Social Security Administration tells us that it operates the Social Security Trust Fund. So it's no shame for an intelligent citizen to think that we already have a giant fund.

So what is the Social Security Trust Fund? To be blunt, until recently it has been a petty cash fund. Each year's benefits to retirees have been financed by current payroll taxes, not earnings from a giant fund. The assets of the Trust Fund have been only a tiny fraction of the liabilities to workers who have contributed. If taxes were ended, the Trust Fund would be able to pay only a tiny fraction of the benefits due these workers.

Here's my proposal. Gradually widen the gap between taxes and benefits so that Social Security runs a substantial surplus each year and a large permanent Social Security fund accumulates over the next few decades. Instruct the Social Security Administration to contract with private firms to invest the fund in a diversified portfolio of stocks and bonds. Exclude Social Security from official reports and targets concerning the federal budget, and from any statute or constitutional amendment requiring a balanced federal budget, so that the federal budget must be balanced not counting the Social Security surpluses. Finally, protect the fund from a raid.

Is my proposal novel? Not at all. Others have advocated accumulating a large permanent Social Security fund. We've already begun to accumulate a genuine Social Security fund under the pathbreaking Social Security reform of 1983. Unfortunately, the current buildup has four shortcomings: It is not large enough; the fund is currently invested solely in low-yield government bonds; Social Security is currently included in official reports and targets concerning the federal budget; and the fund is inadequately protected against a raid. Let me tell you about my proposals for remedying each defect.

Increase the Fund Buildup

Social Security needs a large fund buildup to handle the little problem it faces in the future. You've never heard of this problem? Actually, you've probably heard a lot about it, much of it alarmist. There has been too much irresponsible fear-mongering about Social Security. The Social Security system has a problem, not a crisis. It will not collapse. You will receive a benefit when you retire. There, I hope you feel better.

But there is a problem. Why? In the absence of a large fund, each year Social Security must rely solely on current payroll tax revenue to pay benefits. This is called "pay-as-you-go" (PAYGO) finance, and it was used by Social Security in its first half century. PAYGO is a good deal for retirees for a few decades after it starts, because the retirees get benefits over their entire retirement even though they paid taxes only during the last part of their work career. But after a few decades, new retirees have paid taxes their entire work life, and PAYGO is no longer a very good deal.

What determines how good a deal PAYGO is? Two things. First, labor force growth. The more workers per retiree, the more payroll tax revenue raised per retiree. Second, real (inflation-adjusted) wage growth. The higher the wage, the more revenue raised by the payroll tax, per retiree.

Unfortunately, these two elements do not look good for the baby boomers who will be retiring in the decades near 2020. While a lot of baby boomers will reach retirement around then, there won't be as many following behind them, so that the number of workers per retiree will fall. In addition, productivity growth, which determines real wage growth, has been low.

But even after the baby boomers are gone, it can be shown that the return under PAYGO will on average equal the sum of the population growth rate and the real wage (or productivity) growth rate. Population growth may well be 0 percent in economically advanced countries like the United States, and productivity growth is likely to be about 2 percent, so the real (inflation-adjusted) return under PAYGO Social Security will probably average 2 percent after the boomers, and less than that for the boomers. By contrast, if the compulsory saving (taxes) of workers were invested in a diversified portfolio of corporate stocks and bonds, and government bonds, it would on average probably yield a real (inflation-adjusted) return of roughly 4 percent. The reason is that the returns on corporate stock returns usually reflect the returns of the business investment they finance, and have averaged roughly 6 percent, while the yield on government bonds has been about 2 percent. So a mixed portfolio should yield a real (inflation-adjusted) return of about 4 percent, twice the return that can be expected with PAYGO financing. Doubling the return makes an enormous difference over a lifetime.

So what will happen without my proposal? A dramatic collapse? Not at all. Instead, Congress will either cut the Social Security *replacement rate* so that the average retiree's benefit will be a smaller fraction of his pre-retirement wage than it is today, or payroll tax rates will be raised several points higher than they are today. Most likely, a combination of both measures will be taken.

There will be an unpleasant intergenerational tug-of-war fought out in Congress, with lobbying by the old against benefit cuts and lobbying by the young against payroll tax hikes. Congress will compromise, and neither side will be happy. There will be no collapse, but there will be much bad feeling, and much dissatisfaction with Social Security.

Two questions will naturally arise in 2020: Why do we, the retirees of 2020, deserve a replacement rate much smaller than the retirees of 2000? And why do we, the workers of 2020, deserve payroll tax rates much higher than the workers of 2000? Good questions. Why should Social Security treat the retirees and workers of 2000 much differently from the retirees and workers of 2020?

The accumulation of a large Social Security fund between 2000 and 2020 is a fairer way to divide the burden between the populations of 2000 and 2020. The annual investment income on a large fund can help bridge the projected gap between benefits and payroll taxes in 2020, so there need not be as large a cut in the replacement rate or increase in the payroll tax rate. Today's population will bear an additional burden—releasing the revenue to build the fund—in order to reduce the burden on the population of 2020.

But even beyond 2020, workers will always be justifiably unhappy if corporate stocks on average yield a return of 6 percent while PAYGO Social Security yields only 2 percent. Although it is too risky for the Social Security portfolio to hold only corporate stocks, a diversified portfolio with a mix of corporate stocks, corporate bonds, and government bonds would probably yield a real (inflation-adjusted) return of 4 percent with very low risk.

I suspect you are wondering why Social Security experts have not thought of this. The answer is, they have. This fund buildup is just what the bipartisan Social Security Commission of 1982 recommended, and just what Congress enacted in 1983, launching the fund accumulation that is now under way.

The 1983 reform saw a problem coming, and raised both the payroll tax rate and the earnings ceiling to begin the buildup of the Social Security fund. Under that reform, the fund was supposed to rise gradually to roughly 30 percent of GDP at its peak near 2020—six times annual Social Security benefits—and then fall gradually to zero in about 2050.

Not bad, you say. True enough. But alas, the projections have changed significantly for the worse since then. It is now estimated that the fund will reach a much smaller peak near 2020 and be drawn down to zero by 2030. So from 2020 to 2030, Social Security will significantly reduce national saving as the government bonds in the fund are sold to help pay benefits, and the fund therefore dissaves ("decumulates"). And in 2030, payroll taxes are projected to be only about 75 percent of promised benefits, so in 2030 Congress will be forced to raise taxes and cut benefits, making all ages extremely unhappy.

So my proposal is this: Make the fund even bigger than was originally intended, big enough so that its investment income is sufficient so that the fund itself can be maintained permanently, generating investment income every year to help finance benefits. Social Security with a permanent large fund will be a stronger Social Security. It is better for benefits to depend partly on the fund's investment income and partly on payroll taxes than to depend completely on payroll taxes. It is better for the combined (employer plus employee) payroll tax rate to be less than 6 percent than more than 12 percent (its current rate).

Furthermore, instruct the Social Security Administration to contract with private firms to invest the fund in a diversified portfolio of stocks and bonds. Under current law, the fund can only be invested in low-yield government bonds. Based on history, a diversified portfolio of stocks and bonds would not be very risky, but would yield a return several percentage points higher than government bonds. A diversified portfolio that includes government bonds as well as corporate stocks and bonds would probably yield a real (inflation-adjusted) return of 4 percent with very low risk. It would be judged a good deal by most workers.

Exclude Social Security from the Federal Budget

At present, Social Security is included in reports and targets concerning the federal budget. Why? Because it helps the president and Congress look better. Social Security is now running surpluses and will do so, even if my proposal for a bigger fund is ignored, until about 2020. So including Social Security helps the federal budget look better through 2020. If the budget deficit without Social Security would have been $50 billion, but Social Security runs a surplus of $50 billion, then including Social Security results in the report of a balanced budget.

Does this really matter? If one goal is to raise national saving, it matters crucially. To really boost national saving, we should raise government saving, and this would happen if we run a surplus in the entire federal budget including Social Security. One way to do this is to run a surplus in Social Security, and a balance in the rest of the federal budget. We achieve less saving by running a surplus in the Social Security system if this is canceled by a comparable deficit (dissaving) in the rest of the federal budget.

To be fair, there is a respectable argument for including Social Security in the federal budget. In order to judge the impact of federal fiscal policy on the economy, we do need to consider all federal expenditures and revenues, including Social Security. Actually, best of all might be to keep Social Security in the budget, but then aim for a budget surplus rather than balance.

Alas, the best is sometimes the enemy of the good. A balanced budget target has the virtue of simplicity, and simplicity can help to discipline politicians. It is doubtful that a budget goal of an X percent surplus, instead of balance, can be made to stick. It's hard to imagine that a citizens' movement could hold Congress to achieving a budget surplus of say, 2 percent of GDP. After all, why 2 percent? But however shaky its underpinnings in theoretical economics, the goal of a balanced budget—a zero deficit—has a natural magnetism for the electorate. That reality is important for the chances of holding Congress's feet to the fire.

So, on practical grounds, it is better to move Social Security off-budget, require balance in the rest of the budget, and build the surplus within Social Security. But why, you reasonably ask, should there be a better chance of achieving a surplus in Social Security than in the whole federal budget? The reason is that the baby boom retirement problem of the next century creates a tangible justification for accumulating a large Social Security fund. Without the earnings of a large fund to help bridge the projected gap between benefits and payroll tax revenues next century, either the replacement rate will be cut sharply or the payroll tax rate will be raised significantly. Social Security's special problem provides a justification for running surpluses that citizens and politicians can easily grasp.

Protecting the Fund

Unfortunately, the Social Security fund that is now building up is inadequately protected from a raid. "What's a raid?" you ask. We must now speak candidly about an important practical objection to building up the Social Security fund. Imagine it is the year 2010. A healthy fund has been accumulated. It will generate investment income each year that can help finance benefits. This investment income will be especially important when the baby boomers soon retire. But the Congress of 2010 eyes the fund greedily. Why not draw down the fund now and immediately raise benefits?

Raiding of the fund will always be popular with current retirees. The key to deterring a raid is to make sure that current workers realize that it is their future benefits that are being raided. If the fund is drawn down, then its investment income will be lower in future years, and so will Social Security benefits. But how can millions of workers be aroused to oppose a raid?

Suppose the Social Security system is required to send each worker an annual estimate of his expected retirement benefit, based on current tax rates, benefit rules, and the size of the fund and its investment income. A raid on the fund this year would reduce each worker's expected benefit in next year's annual statement. Every congressman who votes for a raid would know that workers in his district will soon learn the impact of his vote on their own expected benefit. It may be somewhat abstract for a worker to learn from the media that Congress has raided the Social Security fund. But it is bound to be a moving, personal experience when he connects the media story to the specific dollar reduction on his annual statement.

The annual statement is a good thing in itself. Today, most workers have little idea of how much to expect from Social Security. An annual statement is worthwhile just to help people figure out how much they need to save for retirement. But the statement would also be an important obstacle to a congressional raid on the Social Security fund.

Where Will the Annual Surpluses Come From?

Now we come to the unpleasant part. To achieve a surplus initially, Social Security taxes must be set higher than benefits. Remember that in a growing economy, taxes and benefits per person grow each year. For our purpose of raising the national saving rate, it doesn't matter whether tax growth is accelerated or benefit growth is decelerated. All that matters is that a gap is achieved without disturbing the required balance in the rest of the federal budget.

Neither faster tax growth nor slower benefit growth is likely to win any popularity awards. This should come as no surprise. The effect is to raise the national saving rate; by definition, this requires reducing the national consumption rate. That means, alas, that consumption growth must be slowed either for taxpayers or for benefit recipients. There is no escape from this somber conclusion.

Here's how to minimize the pain. The temporary slowdown in benefit growth and the temporary tax increase should both be phased in gradually, and low-income workers should be protected by an expansion of the earned income tax credit (discussed in chapter 12). The temporary increase in the payroll tax rate will be only a few percentage points. Then as the fund's investment income grows, the tax rate will gradually and permanently be cut more than in half (from over 12 percent to under 6 percent) and benefit growth will be returned to normal.

One Social Security Fund vs. Many Individual Funds

Why not require each worker to build his own fund, instead of building up a single Social Security fund? This proposal is called *privatization.*

Of course, building many individual funds is just as painful as building one big fund. If the federal government must keep the rest of its budget balanced and meet its obligation to current and future retirees who have paid Social Security taxes all their lives, then it must replace the payroll tax revenue that each worker now sends to his own fund. It can do this only by cutting spending or raising taxes.

This point about the pain in privatization deserves emphasis. A few advocates enjoy asking young workers: "Wouldn't you rather invest several thousand dollars a year in your own fund than send it to the government for Social Security?" Young workers often say yes. But honest advocates of privatization immediately point out that additional revenue must then be raised to meet our obligations to current and future retirees who have paid taxes under our Social Security system. Once this point is made, privatization is seen to be as painful as building up a single Social Security fund.

Once we recognize that each involves similar transitional pain, we are ready to address the question, "So which is better: a single large fund, or many individual funds?" An important advantage of a single fund is that the stock and bond market risk is pooled for all retirees. Privatization advocates worry about government administrators, or even politicians, influencing the choice of stocks and bonds held by a single Social Security fund. But I propose that the Social Security Administration contract with several private firms to invest in a diversified portfolio of stocks and bonds. It should not be hard to insulate the private management of these diversified portfolios from political influence.

Another advantage of the single fund is that it enables some redistribution. Under Social Security's progressive benefit formula, there is some redistribution from high-wage to low-wage workers when they retire: If person H earned three times the wage and paid three times the tax each year as person L, person H will receive a benefit perhaps twice but not three times as great as person L because of the progressive benefit formula. By contrast, with individual funds, if person H earned three times the wage as person L, person H will receive a benefit approximately three times as great as person L.

Still another advantage of a single fund is that workers with the same wage histories will receive the same benefits. By contrast, with many individual funds, workers with the same wage histories will receive different benefits because returns will vary among funds; one fund's portfolio may soar in value, while another's may plummet. Some workers will obtain exceptional benefits; others will be destitute in old age, dependent on the welfare system for survival.

Should workers be free to risk destitution in old age? Some will say yes, others no. Before the fact, a young person may say yes. After the fact, that same person, now old, may say no. Here's my personal view. Risk-taking is good for the health of the economy—up to a point. We certainly don't want everyone guaranteed, as well as limited to, an average income. We want individuals to consider risky options, where they can strike it big or end up well below average. On the other hand, I think we ought to discourage the all-or-none gamble played by the young person, lived by the old one.

So my preference is for a single Social Security fund where the stock and bond market risk is pooled among all retirees, the fund is managed by private firms under contract with the Social Security Administration, and a progressive benefit formula assures a decent retirement for everyone. Beyond that, let people take individual risks on private saving and career choice. And, as advocated in chapter 3, let the personal consumption tax replace the personal income tax to encourage this additional saving. Let's gradually fund Social Security, not privatize it.

Conclusion

It is possible to raise the national saving rate and to handle Social Security's 2020 problem at the same time. We can do this by running a substantial surplus each year in the Social Security system for the next few decades while excluding Social Security from the balanced budget statute, and having the Social Security Administration contract with private firms to invest the fund in a diversified portfolio of stocks and bonds. The surplus will then represent a genuine increase in national saving. Once a large permanent fund accumulates, its investment income will help bridge the projected gap between Social Security benefits and tax revenues when the baby boomers retire next century; and after the baby boomers are gone, *funded Social Security* will be a better deal for future workers than PAYGO Social Security.

10 HEALTH CARD

President Competitus had reason to be proud. His policies had kept the United States second to none economically. As his plane touched down in Stockholm for a meeting of economically advanced nations, he was radiant, eager for the press conference that would soon follow.

"What will they ask about first?" he said to his coterie of confident aides. "Will it be about our recent success in raising our saving rate? I can't wait."

As he entered the airport, the president was pleased to see the throng of foreign reporters, pushing and shoving to get near the microphone he would use for his press conference. Soon he was behind the microphone, smiling confidently.

"Ladies and gentlemen, I would be delighted to answer your questions."

"Mr. President," said a Swedish reporter, "why is it that your nation—among the richest on earth—permits thousands of citizens to be financially broken by medical bills, and millions to worry that the same thing might happen to them?"

For an instant, President Competitus was taken aback. He had not expected this question. But he recovered quickly.

"In the United States we believe that doctors and hospitals shouldn't be strangled by government regulation. We believe they should be free to practice medicine without government interference."

"Perhaps so," responded the reporter, "but my question was about paying bills, not the free practice of medicine. Why doesn't every citizen have enough health insurance to prevent financial disaster?"

President Competitus tried to remain unruffled. "We have a fine private health insurance system. Many of our citizens obtain free hospital care."

But the reporter persisted. "I agree that your system takes care of the average person's routine hospital stay. But what about the exceptionally long hospital stay? Or the person with a chronic illness who needs outpatient and home care? And what about the person who is not average—for example, the person who works for a small business that doesn't provide health insurance, or the person who is between jobs and has no coverage? Isn't it true, Mr. President, that your system permits these citizens to suffer an unbearable financial burden due to a medical problem?"

The color was draining from President Competitus's face. He looked around for help. At that moment an aide earned his pay; he calmly took the microphone and said, "The president would love to entertain more questions, but I'm afraid we are already late for our reception. There will be time for questions tomorrow. Thank you very much."

With that, the aide unplugged the microphone and led the president by the arm away from the throng. A half hour later, the president huddled with his advisers in a hotel suite high above Stockholm. He knew he would have to face the reporters again the next day.

"These Scandinavians are so darn righteous about their welfare state, especially about medical care. But maybe they're right," he said. "Maybe medical care should be free for everyone. Maybe our government should pay everyone's entire medical bill."

It happened that the president's inner circle included a health economist who, needless to say, immediately spoke up.

"Mr. President, that would be a serious mistake. I agree that our lack of universal protection against financial disaster is shameful. But we shouldn't go to the other extreme. After all, you do remember the Aroman Food Crisis, don't you?"

"The Aroman Food Crisis?" everyone asked all at once. No one had ever heard of it. From his briefcase, the health economist pulled out what appeared to be an old manuscript.

"The hour is late," he said. "Tomorrow morning we can begin to develop a national policy for health insurance. Tonight, relax, and let me read to you from this ancient text. I assure you it will prove helpful when we get down to business tomorrow morning."

And so he began to read.

The Aroman Food Crisis

I

An ancient proverb warns, "There is no such thing as a free lunch." Yet many years ago, in the land of Aroma, there emerged a free-wheeling, spirited, well-intentioned people, confident that food could, and should, be free. On a historic day, the Aroman Senate rose to its finest hour and passed the long-awaited Free Food Act. Lest the title mislead you, in a dramatic amendment before final passage, Senator Inebriatus, with an impassioned though rambling oration, won the inclusion of all beverages under the act.

The passage of the Free Food Act (FFA) had been inspired by the tragic plight of those Aromans with enormous nutritional requirements—fortunately, only a small fraction of the citizenry. But when the Senate's work was done, the act had gone well beyond these citizens. For under the act, food and drink were free for all Aromans. No longer would any Aroman face even the smallest "barrier" to food and drink. In other words, no longer would any Aroman have to pay for what he consumed.

Never again would any Aroman be seen in the marketplace trying to decide whether a luscious honeydew melon was worth its price. Nor would the marketplace be degraded by haggling and bargaining between stubborn buyers and sellers. Now, there would only be smiles. "Take as much as you want," was the refrain that abounded. "My price is not for you, my friend, but for our beloved government." Word spread to other lands about the pleasant vibrations of the Aroman marketplace.

Yet it was not the gaiety of the marketplace that caused the most excitement in distant lands. Most wondrous of all were the spectacular public banquets that soon became an everyday feature of Aroman life. Soon after the FFA was passed, banquet halls sprang up throughout Aroma. Aromans had always taken a large midday meal. But now, in retrospect, those meals seemed like a quick snack by comparison.

Each banquet hall manager boasted of serving only the finest, regardless of cost. When one government regulator asked the manager of the Endless Lobster, perhaps the most renowned hall in all Aroma, if perhaps his place was not a bit extravagant, the manager's reply was angry: "Are you suggesting that I sacrifice quality? I would rather be banished from Aroma than offer second-class food and drink." The government regulator was reported to have hung his head in shame and then apologized profusely.

And so, the early days of the Free Food Act were joyous, heady ones for the Aromans.

II

But alas, this happy Aroman scene did not last long. Indeed, to the dismay of many Aromans, the country was soon on the brink of disaster. While food and drink were free to each Aroman, someone, of course, had to pay the bill. Now, it was no surprise to the average Aroman that it was the government who was supposed to pay food sellers in the marketplace and the banquet halls. Indeed, it was the cry, "The government should pay!" that rang in the ears of Aroman senators when they passed the FFA.

What surprised the average Aroman was the government's an-
nouncement that, in order to honor its financial obligations to the
food providers, it would have to raise the taxes of each Aroman
citizen.

Even more shocking than the imposition of the new Food Tax
was its astounding size. The tax came to five times as much per
meal per person as the average Aroman had spent before the FFA.
The reason, said the government spokesman, was simple: the average Aroman was now selecting food and drink of such quality
and quantity that the cost per meal was now five times as great.

The Aroman Senate responded to the crisis. It held hearings on
the Incredible Overutilization, as it was called. So vivid were the
accounts of the banquet hall abuses that senators were regularly
given the ancient potion Alka-Seltzer. In angry testimony, taxpayers testified that banquet hall managers did nothing to control
costs. They simply passed their exorbitant expenses on to the
government, which reimbursed them, no questions asked.

Amid the furor, the Senate acted. The answer, said the committee report, was to negotiate prices, and establish a limited
budget, in advance, with each banquet hall and food seller.

"Since we are spending five times as much on food and drink
as we should be," stated the Senate committee report, "we will
simply appropriate only one-fifth of our current expenditure.
Within this limit, we will allocate our budget on a regional basis.
In each region, we will enter into agreements with each food
provider. Once agreement is reached, the banquet hall will get no
more than the amount specified in the agreement for the year, no
matter how great its costs.

"With a firm regulatory hand," the report concluded, "we will
control costs without retreating from the sacred principle that the
individual must face absolutely no financial barrier to food and
drink."

On leaving the Senate chamber, one senator said with a confident smile, "If we refuse to appropriate any more money, then we
can't spend more, can we? The food cost crisis is over."

III

But the trouble was only beginning. Yes, the expenditure ceiling ended the cost crisis. But it produced a crisis that many Aromans felt was far worse. As the end of the fiscal year approached, food for the country nearly ran out. Aromans were faced with starvation. How did it happen?

It happened because banquet halls and food suppliers reached their negotiated limits well before the year was over. Except for the price control and a budget ceiling on each provider, the new amendment changed nothing else. Aromans continued to order the finest food and drink. With food still free to each Aroman, there was no reason for the average Aroman to change his behavior. Aroman waiters continued to encourage the highest quality, regardless of cost. As for the banquet hall managers, they looked forward to a fine vacation during the last months of the year.

"I can reach my reimbursement ceiling in nine months," said one banquet manager. "Why should I reduce our quality and style? My customers want the finest, in abundant quantities, and I am proud to satisfy them. Let someone else plan for the end of the year. I and my fine professional staff will enjoy a well-earned vacation."

After a gluttonous fall and winter, Aromans struggled through the spring near starvation, desperately awaiting the new fiscal year, which in those days began in July. Many affluent Aromans were still able to obtain food, thanks to an illegal market. Aroman entrepreneurs, anticipating the shortage, had stockpiled free food during the fall and winter, and now sold it at high prices to those able to pay. But many other Aromans suffered. Meanwhile, new hearings were held in the Senate, where the mood was one of sober realism.

"It is obvious," said one senator, "that unless we directly control the practice of each food seller and banquet hall, budget ceilings will continue to produce disaster. We cannot limit the total expenditure unless we also carefully control the individual expenditures that eventually constitute the total."

It was now clear that the annual budget negotiation with each provider would have to become detailed, indeed. The provider's entire mode of operation would have to be carefully scrutinized before the ceiling was fixed. Each provider would have to be kept under constant surveillance to make sure that it complied with the budget agreement. But how could this be done effectively?

"We need to review utilization at each banquet hall," asserted one senator. "If they keep serving expensive food and liquor, we'll threaten to cut off their funds."

This was met by a disdainful glare from the chefs and waiters in the gallery. Then Intimidatus, the president of the Aroman Maitre d's Association (AMA), which also represented chefs and ordinary waiters, addressed the Senate committee. His dignified manner and white hair, seeming to symbolize wisdom and responsibility, filled the Senate with awe. Intimidatus calmly pointed out that many of the items on the menus of the finest banquet halls were modern nutritional necessities.

He then referred to these items, analyzing each, leaving the senators confused, but impressed with his abstruse terminology. "Yes, in some cases they are not necessary, and may even be harmful. But in others, the very life of the individual is at stake. If laymen are allowed to interfere with the professional judgment of trained waiters who advise citizens what to order, lives will be jeopardized."

Needless to say, a chill ran through the Senate chamber. "You waiters and chefs who are properly trained in nutrition," Senator Conciliatus blurted out, "are the only ones qualified to judge what each individual requires. Only you can separate unnecessary overutilization from genuine necessity. I therefore propose that we establish Professional Standards Review Organizations in each area. Let's call them PSROs. They will be composed exclusively of trained waiters and chefs, who will review the practices of each banquet hall. The PSRO will recommend when funds should be cut because waste is occurring." The proposal was greeted enthusiastically by other senators.

Their glee was interrupted, however, when the president of the AMA asked, "I trust that the PSRO will also be charged with making sure that the highest quality standards are preserved at all banquet halls?" While the senators nodded uneasily, they wondered whether a PSRO would try to keep cost down as much as it would try to keep quality and style up. "What would you concentrate on if you were a chef or waiter on a PSRO?" one senator asked another nervously.

"The trouble with the PSRO," said Senator Consumus, rising to his feet, "is that it has only waiters and chefs. Of course it won't be tough enough. We need strong consumer representation on these review boards. Then we'll get action."

IV

For the first time since the debate began, Senator Economus asked to be recognized. "Consumus, how carefully will your board review each case, and how many will they examine?"

"Oh," replied Consumus, "they will surely review most cases, and each very carefully."

"Surely, Consumus, you realize what that would cost? There are thousands of cases. We would be wasting an important fraction of our labor force serving on review boards, instead of producing goods and services."

Though momentarily dismayed, Consumus quickly regained his composure. "Well, then they will review only a small number of cases, but will do these carefully. After all, this is the method of our respected Internal Revenue Service. The fear of review will make all waiters act properly."

"I'm afraid that there is a basic difference between the taxpayer and the waiter," responded Economus. "For the taxpayer, there is relatively little discretion. The rules say what he must count as his income, and what he must pay. If he is caught with a major discrepancy, he may argue, but almost always to no avail. Our IRS will not hesitate to punish him when his crime is clear. It is this willingness to punish because the crime is clear that makes our taxpayers afraid, and makes most of them comply without our direct oversight.

"Our waiter," Economus continued, "is in a very different position. Only in the most scandalous cases will his actions clearly be a crime. With so much judgment involved in serving an individual's nutritional needs, with even our most expert waiters disagreeing over what is most appropriate, punishment in most cases would be most unfair. In the overwhelming majority of cases, therefore, the review board will at most reprimand the waiter, and warn against future excesses. Do you think most waiters will change their ways because there is a small chance that they might be slapped on the wrist?"

An expression of gloom came over the senators' faces.

Consumus grew more flustered. "Then the board will have to show the courage to impose a severe penalty. If the description of the case looks suspicious, the board will just have to act."

At this, Economus rose to his feet. "Are you saying, Consumus, that if a waiter and his customer, based on the particular nutritional history and needs of this customer, after extensive consultation and examination, decide that certain food and drink are necessary, that your board, based on a descriptive account, will overrule their decision?"

"How else will we get results?" replied Consumus with exasperation. "Of course, they will have the right to appeal."

"But," continued Economus, "if your appeal board conducts a careful investigation, this will once again be very expensive. Virtually everyone will appeal, since much is at stake. If your appeal board processes cases without such investigation, and at low cost, it will be little better than the review board in the first place. An outside board, with far less information about the customer's special needs, will impose its decision on the customer and waiter."

"Well," replied Consumus, "what's so wrong with that? As long as consumers constitute a majority on the board, they'll watch out for the customer's needs. After all, how can consumer representatives be harmful to individual consumers?"

"By not having sufficient on-the-scene information, Consumus, to make the decision with the sensitivity that is required. Yes, they may be right some of the time, when excessive food and drink has been ordered. But what about the other cases, where what was ordered was truly necessary, but the review board is simply unable to investigate carefully enough to realize this? I suppose those individuals, with perhaps their very lives at stake, are just out of luck."

"That's the price we'll have to pay," Consumus responded, defiant yet uneasy.

Another senator now turned to a different aspect of the problem. "We are building too many banquet halls, with facilities and equipment that are far too extravagant for our needs. This must end." His plea obviously struck a responsive chord. "I propose," he continued, "that every new banquet hall, and every expansion of a current one, be required to obtain a Certificate of Need from the government before it can proceed."

Economus slowly rose to his feet. "You will do more harm than good if you limit facilities and equipment without changing individual utilization. It's the same as thinking that a spending ceiling can end the problem."

"But why?" asked Senator Naivus. Other senators turned uneasily to hear Economus's explanation, glad that Senator Naivus, as usual, had asked the question for them.

"Suppose," began Economus, "that according to your rational planning, you think there are already enough banquet halls, kitchen facilities, and so on, in some area. How did you decide this? By calculating how much would be needed if each person ate reasonably, and only those with special nutritional requirements ordered expensive food. But suppose people don't eat reasonably. Suppose they continue to eat and drink the way they are doing today. Then you'll run out of capacity, under your plan, and we'll have another emergency. Some of our people will wine and dine extravagantly, as usual. But many others won't be able to get a table at any banquet hall, because there will be no room. And someone who truly needs a special food will find that the special kitchen facilities are being used to prepare that food for someone who is ordering it as a luxury."

Most dismayed by what Economus said was Senator Regulatus. He countered, "Economus, if our ability to regulate is really so feeble, then why are our people satisfied with our great public utilities, which my committee oversees? For example, our water utility company distributes water, and our fuel utility company fuel, to every Aroman home. We regulate the price each charges, and few citizens complain."

"What you are forgetting," Economus answered, "is that every Aroman home must pay for the water and fuel it consumes. So people only use what they need, and no more. That's why there is no serious problem. With our utility companies, we have to regulate the price they charge, because they're monopolies. But we don't have to regulate utilization, because people do that themselves since they have to pay for whatever they use. That's the crucial difference."

After a long silence in the chamber, another senator asked the final question to Economus. "Are you saying that trying to regulate efficiency through utilization review, certificate of need, spending ceilings, prospective reimbursement, and other requirements may well do more harm than good?"

"That is exactly what I'm saying," Economus replied.

V

"If we can't regulate banquet halls and marketplace food stands," said Senator Socialus, "then let's take them over and run them ourselves, on behalf of the people." Proposals by Senator Socialus were usually viewed with suspicion by other senators. But now, out of desperation, they listened. "First, we'll put all the chefs, waiters, and maitre d's on salary, and stop paying them in proportion to the cost of the food and drink they serve. That will end their incentive to encourage over-ordering." Many senators nodded, and Socialus continued. "We'll have rational planning of facilities and food production. This is the only way we can solve our problem." While the proposal was radical, many senators seemed to feel it might be the only course left.

But then Economus spoke up. "How will the budget for a banquet hall, and the salaries of those who run them, be determined?"

Socialus answered, "Our government will decide these matters on behalf of the people. We will create a Ministry of Food and Drink to administer this sector of our economy."

Economus responded, "If the Ministry of Food and Drink, rather than consumers, determines the financial success of these providers, then it is the Ministry, not their customers, that they will have an incentive to please."

"But Economus," replied Socialus, "the Ministry will only reward providers who please their customers."

"How will the Ministry know who these are?" Economus asked.

"Well," answered Socialus, "we might take surveys of customers. Or better yet, we could see which providers are greatly in demand and which are not."

"There is a problem with your method," said Economus. "Since consumers pay nothing, they will prefer the banquet halls and food stands where they are allowed to order as much as they want. The most popular providers will probably be the most wasteful. Surely you will not reward their popularity with higher budgets and salaries."

"Of course not," Socialus responded, "but we will evaluate them, don't you worry."

"Then I must repeat," said Economus, "that it will be the evaluators, not customers, whom each provider will be most eager to please. This raises a still more serious problem. Do you realize how many banquet halls and food stands there are in Aroma?"

"Thousands of them," interrupted Naivus, who had been listening intently, along with the other senators.

"How will the Ministry oversee, evaluate, and administer all of these efficiently?" continued Economus.

"Why, the Ministry will have to be given the manpower it

needs to do the job. We must have administrators in each local community who will be responsible for all providers in that area.

They will in turn report to regional administrators, who in turn will report to the Ministry itself. We will have constant communication between the bottom and top of our hierarchy."

"Have you estimated the cost of employing these full-time administrators?" asked Economus.

"No," answered Socialus, "but the cost of justice is surely worth bearing."

"Unless the same justice can be achieved far more cheaply," replied Economus, continuing to warm to his topic. "When it is budget time, will your local administrators be advocates for their providers or representatives of the Ministry?"

"They will represent the Ministry, of course," answered Socialus. "They must recommend that their superior providers be rewarded and the inferior ones penalized."

"Are you sure it will not work the other way around?" said Economus. "For example, if most of the providers in an area do a poor job, do you really expect the administrator to recommend that funds for his area be cut?" Socialus replied saying yes, this was the administrator's duty. Economus continued, "There is a problem here. If you do not reward area administrators according to the performance of their providers, what incentive do they have to strive to improve service in their area? On the other hand, if you do reward them on that basis, they will have an incentive to become advocates for their providers, defending their performance before the Ministry. You will have great difficulty judging provider performance."

"Economus, your trouble is that you always assume financial incentives are everything. Our administrators will realize that they are servants of the people. They will act accordingly, and strive to make the system work for people's needs."

"Socialus, my good friend, I do not think that financial incentives are everything. But I'm afraid I have seen too much in my time to agree with you that they are nothing. And there is something else about your plan that disturbs me," continued Economus. "Suppose an area has a poor administrator, and providers in that area give poor service. They are discourteous to customers, whom they have little incentive to please as long as the budget keeps funding them; they often keep people waiting in lines for tables, and offer a poor assortment of low-quality dishes. Socialus, what recourse do the people of this area have?"

"I expected a more difficult problem, my dear Economus," answered Socialus confidently. "Obviously, they can complain to the Ministry. In fact, we will do better. In each area, we will set up consumer councils. It will be their responsibility to take the complaints of citizens to the Ministry. Citizens will have the opportunity, at last, to participate directly in governing the institutions that control their lives."

"I'm afraid, my dear Socialus, that your answer does not satisfy me. Surely, this will be a time-consuming process. The administrators and providers will defend themselves. It will require a sustained campaign by local citizens and their councils to achieve results. Perhaps some citizens will enjoy the battle. The vast majority, however, want nothing more than good service. Indeed, they do not wish to spend their time attending consumer council meetings, or writing letters to the Ministry."

"Then they must learn to like direct participation and the democratic process," replied Socialus.

"In the meantime," Economus went on, "until they have won a change, these unlucky Aromans will have nowhere to turn. Socialus, there is something most ironic here. You are famous for your reputation as an ardent foe of private monopolies, which leave consumers no choice. And yet your plan would turn our whole food and drink sector into one giant monopoly. To be sure, it would be a public monopoly. But like any monopoly, dissatisfied consumers would have nowhere to go."

"Economus, are you unable to see the difference between a private monopoly whose motive is greed and a Ministry whose wish is to serve the people?"

"I see how, in one respect, they are different," Economus replied. "But Socialus, can you see how, in another respect, they are also the same?"

Seeing that this question was in vain, Economus now proceeded to his final point.

"I have a final concern about your proposal, Socialus. It applies not only to your plan, however, but to any Free Food Act that would finance all purchases of food and drink through our government budget. Of all the arguments I have made in the course of this Senate debate, I believe this one may be the most telling of all. You see, so far my arguments for efficiency have struck some of you as lacking in compassion, and perhaps have therefore left you cold. What I am about to say, however, should at last impress those of you whose sole concern is social justice. For I will now explain why, contrary to the humanitarian intentions of the supporters of the Free Food Act, its effects will be to harm, not help, those Aromans whose needs are greatest—our poor and our elderly."

A silence fell on the Senate chamber. Loyal supporters of the Free Food Act, famed for their devotion to programs for the poor and the elderly, turned their attention to Economus for the first time, their countenances reflecting disbelief and concern. The debate had clearly reached its climax, and Economus's ability to defend his assertion seemed likely to decide the outcome.

"As you know," he continued solemnly, "our citizens are unwilling to be taxed without limit. In a dictatorship, where the ruler decides the taxes and people pay them without a whimper for fear of the ruler's wrath, people's sentiments would be no obstacle. But in our Aroman democracy, the situation is very different. We senators must heed the people's wishes, or soon find that others have been elected to replace us.

"Before passing this act, no taxes were needed to finance food and drink. We could therefore devote the taxes we raised to tasks that only our government can effectively perform—like helping our poor and our elderly. If we must now use taxes to finance all food and drink expenditures—an enormous sum—then we will be unable to continue these vital tasks with the same generosity.

It is our poor, and our elderly, who will be harmed the most by the reduction in our other government expenditures. Surely the senators who support full tax financing of food and drink do not realize that its unintended effect would be to shift government spending away from the poor and elderly toward middle- and upper-income Aromans, most of whom can afford to pay their own food bills. I am afraid that the Free Food Act is a sad example of how good intentions can at times lead to harmful results."

A long and sober silence was finally broken by the sound of the gavel of the president of the Senate as he adjourned the session.

VI

When the session opened the next day, Naivus was the first to speak. "What shall we do, Economus?" he asked. As usual, he voiced the question then on the minds of most senators.

"My proposal is very simple," answered Economus, "and I am only too glad to set it before you today. First, we must have compassion for those unfortunate Aromans who have enormous nutritional requirements, and simply cannot afford to pay for most of the food and drink they need. We should place a limit, that varies according to the citizen's income, on the out-of-pocket expense that any Aroman must pay for the food and drink he requires. Once a person reaches the limit, our Aroman government should pay the rest. However, the limit would be set high enough so that only those with truly serious needs would reach it. Let's call my proposal *food insurance.*

"It could be easily implemented through our personal income tax. When an Aroman files his annual income tax return, he reports his annual income to our IRS. Using this information, our government can decide each Aroman's maximum burden. For convenience, our government will initially pay every food bill. When an Aroman buys food, he will simply use a government food credit card with his stamped Social Security number. The provider will send the bill to the government for payment. But then the government will immediately bill the Aroman for the amount he owes, according to his income.

"Fortunately, only a relatively small fraction of Aromans are forced to spend more than that critical fraction of their income on food and drink. Thus, the amount of tax we must raise to help these Aromans is much smaller than the amount required by the Free Food Act. We will therefore be able to continue, and even increase, our government programs to assist the poor and the elderly.

"At the same time, waste and inefficiency will be greatly reduced. Once again, the average Aroman will want to weigh the benefit of anything he orders against its cost. This will automatically limit wasteful over-ordering, without regulation.

"True, Aromans will continue to rely on trained waiters to advise them concerning their nutritional needs, and the food and beverages they require. But our citizens will now communicate to their waiters their concern that the cost be reasonable. Waiters will realize that citizens who incur an excessive food bill will be less able to afford a generous tip. Moreover, citizens will seek waiters who show concern for their pocketbook, as well as their nutrition. Waiters who indulge their 'technological imperative'— who recommend the most technologically sophisticated food preparation without regard to cost or true necessity—will find themselves losing customers. Managers and waiters at extravagant banquet halls will watch, with dismay, as citizens seek prudent waiters at rival halls that provide sufficient quality at far less cost.

"Thus, under my simple proposal, no Aroman will be bankrupted by his nutritional requirements; waste and inefficiency will be largely curtailed without cumbersome and costly regulation; and we will conserve scarce tax dollars so that they can be spent to assist the poor and the elderly in other ways."

When Economus had said this, he thanked the senators for listening, and sat down.

Unfortunately, here the tattered manuscript recounting the Aroman food crisis becomes illegible, and to this day we do not know whether the Aroman senate followed his advice.

Having completed his recounting of the ancient story, the president's health economist looked up. Everyone was sound asleep except the president, who nodded his head drowsily with a sign of approval. Within seconds, he too was asleep.

Health Card

The next morning, the president asked what to do about medical coverage, and his health economist gave this response.

"Mr. President, propose a new kind of national health insurance called *Health Card*. Health Card would utilize a government issued health credit card and the income tax return data of the Internal Revenue Service. It would therefore depend crucially on modern computer technology that would have been unfeasible until recently. Health Card would achieve automatic universal coverage regardless of employment or health status, and cost containment through *equitable* patient cost sharing."

"But how would Health Card work in practice?" asked the President.

His economist replied, "Every household (regardless of employment or health status) would receive a health credit card issued by the federal government. The household would use its health card for medical care the way it uses a MasterCard or Visa card for other goods and services. The medical provider would send a patient's bill to the government's agent (a private credit card company such as Visa or MasterCard, or an insurance company such as Blue Cross/Blue Shield), who would fully pay the provider's bill using government funds. The government's agent would then bill the household for a percentage of its medical bill. This percentage would be scaled to the household's income as reported on its most recent federal income tax return. Once the household's financial burden reaches a designated percentage of its income, it would not be billed again that year, so Health Card

Table 10.1

Health Card Patient Cost Sharing

Income	Cost-sharing rate (%)	Maximum burden (% of income)	Maximum burden ($)	Annual bill causing maximum burden
$ 15,000	5	1.0	$ 150	$ 3,000
$ 30,000	10	2.0	$ 600	$ 6,000
$ 60,000	15	3.0	$1,800	$12,000
$100,000	20	4.0	$4,000	$20,000
$160,000	23	4.6	$7,360	$32,000

would limit every household's financial burden to its ability to pay. Low-income households who owe no income tax would file a short form that would enable them to receive the earned income tax credit as well as their health card. These forms would be available in doctors' offices, hospitals, welfare offices, and post offices. Health Card would replace virtually all private insurance, Medicare, and Medicaid. Table 10.1 illustrates Health Card.

"Like MasterCard or Visa, the government's agent would fully pay the medical provider's bill. If the household's most recent tax return reports an income of $60,000, the agent would bill it 15 percent of its medical bill until its annual medical bill reaches $12,000 and the household's burden reaches $1,800 (15 percent of $12,000), which is 3 percent of its income (3 percent of $60,000); that household would not be billed for any additional medical bill incurred that year, so its maximum burden would be 3 percent of its income. The lower the household's income, the lower would be its patient cost-sharing rate and its maximum burden percentage of income. No matter how affluent, a household's maximum cost-sharing rate would be 25 percent and its maximum burden would be 5 percent of income.

"A Health Card table with finer gradations would be included in the 1040 federal income tax booklet along with the usual tax rate tables. Income would be 'total income' (not taxable income) on the federal income tax return. If a household had an unusually high burden last year, this year's maximum burden and cost-sharing rate would be reduced in order to give further protection to any household with a chronic high-cost medical problem."

"How ironic," noted the president, "that Health Card's fairness depends on using tax return data from the Internal Revenue Service, surely not our most popular government agency."

"Yes, the IRS is perhaps an unlikely hero," replied the health economist. "But Health Card shows the folly of trying to abolish the IRS and do away with the personal (household) tax."

"But," asked the President, "what happens if we convert our personal income tax to a personal consumption tax?"

"That's easy," replied the health economist. "The left column in the table would be consumption instead of income. Health Card would actually be fairer. For retirees, income is a poorer measure of ability to pay than consumption. So converting to a personal consumption tax would improve the fairness of our national health insurance."

"But," said the president, "patients don't want doctors or hospitals to know their income or consumption."

"You're right," replied the health economist. "Health Card would preserve confidentiality concerning each patient's income. Health cards would look alike, just as do MasterCards and Visa cards. Medical providers would not learn their patient's income. The government's agent would pay the full bill for all patients. Each patient's cost-share would be a confidential matter between the government and the patient."

"What about paperwork?" asked the president. "I hear so much complaint about this under our private insurance system."

"Medical providers and patients would appreciate the reduction in paperwork under Health Card," answered the health economist. "Providers would submit bills to a single government agent (the company that obtains the contract for that region through competitive bidding). Patients would periodically pay a

Health Card bill sent by the agent, just as they pay a MasterCard or Visa bill."

"Would all services have the same cost-sharing percentages?" asked the president.

"Not all," replied the health economist. "The government would set the list of covered services under Health Card. Most services would be included at the standard cost-sharing rate. A disputed service might be included at twice, three times, or four times the standard cost-sharing rate, or in the extreme be excluded—that is, require 100 percent patient cost-sharing. For example, if disputed service D were included at twice the cost-sharing rate, then the $60,000 household would bear 30 percent, rather than 15 percent, of its cost. At the same time, certain medical services may be especially encouraged (such as immunizations). Such an encouraged service E might have half, a third, or a fourth of the standard cost-sharing rate. For example, if encouraged service E were included at a third of the cost-sharing rate, then the $60,000 household would bear 5 percent, rather than 15 percent, of its cost. Each household would be provided with a list of services bearing non-standard cost-sharing rates. The list would add some complexity to Health Card and should be adopted only for a minority of services."

"What happens," asked the president, "if a family wants to join a health maintenance organization—an HMO—where the household pays a fixed fee for the year instead of a fee that varies with the cost of its own actual medical service?"

"That's handled easily," answered the health economist. "The Health Card reimbursement schedule, perhaps with some adjustment, would be applied to the HMO fee. For example, if the HMO's monthly premium is $500 ($6,000 for the year)—the $60,000 household would use its Health Card to pay the HMO $500 per month and the government would bill the household $75 (15 percent of $500) per month.

"I'm glad that HMOs fit so easily into Health Card," said the president. "But with HMOs, why do we need Health Card at all? Just last week I met with several HMO advocates. They predicted that most households will soon be enrolled in HMOs or similar prepaid *managed care* organizations. Instead of traditional fee-for-service (FFS), where the doctor or hospital is paid more when more service is provided, the HMO doctor or hospital usually receives a fixed payment regardless of how much service is provided. The HMO advocates said that HMO administrators and doctors will limit service and cost."

"They will," agreed the health economist. "But this may be good or bad, depending on the particular case. True, with FFS, doctors may be tempted to provide an unnecessary, costly service, because then they are paid more. But with a pre-paid HMO, doctors may be tempted to avoid providing a beneficial but costly service, because the HMO will have to absorb the cost."

"I see," said the president. "So with an HMO, there is a risk that doctors will do too little, just as with FFS, there is a risk they will do too much."

"Exactly," said the health economist. "Each family must weigh the risk. I predict that once families begin to realize that HMO doctors may be tempted to do too little, many will decide that they prefer FFS. So HMOs will not be able to stabilize all medical costs because many families will end up choosing fee-for-service doctors and hospitals. Hopefully, a healthy competition between HMO and FFS doctors and hospitals will protect families from excesses—either too much or too little service."

"Will HMOs solve our coverage problem?" asked the president.

"Not at all," replied the health economist. "Since HMOs charge a fixed fee regardless of how much service is provided to a family, HMOs will try their best to avoid families likely to generate high medical costs."

"But can't government compel HMOs to serve everyone?" asked the president.

"How?" asked the health economist. "Government can write regulations and exert pressure. But they can't force HMOs to buy equipment and hire specialists so they can give high quality care to patients with high-cost problems. The HMO will be telling the truth when it tells a high-cost family it cannot handle its case, and the family should seek medical care elsewhere."

"But fee-for-service doctors and hospitals are glad to treat high-cost families," said the president.

"Exactly," replied the health economist. "So that's why we need Health Card. Health Card covers all households automatically, whether they choose FFS or HMO doctors. It guarantees that every household, whether high cost or low cost, will be able to obtain and afford the medical care it needs."

"But," said the president, "Health Card will involve new taxes. How am I going to persuade people to accept new taxes?"

"It won't be as hard as you fear," answered the health economist. "Under Health Card, employers would send checks to the government ('taxes') instead of to private insurance companies ('premiums'). The average employer and employee would hardly notice the change from the current system. Employers would simply send comparable checks to a different address. Either the current Medicare payroll tax could be increased several percentage points and become the Health Card payroll tax, or a value-added tax (VAT) could be enacted and become the Health Card VAT, or a combination of payroll tax and VAT might finance Health Card. The Health Card tax would replace premium expenditures at the typical firm so that employees' take-home pay would be largely unchanged.

"The Health Card tax could be supplemented by a set of health taxes. Health taxes discourage behavior that harms health—such as consuming tobacco, consuming alcohol excessively, or polluting the environment. The health taxes would have three goals: (1) reduce the harmful behavior; (2) make those who engage in such behavior pay for the consequences; (3) raise revenue for Health Card.

"National health expenditure is roughly 15 percent of gross domestic product (GDP). Health Card would impose the same 15 percent burden through different channels. Under current arrangements, roughly 5 percent is paid by private insurers, 5 percent by the federal government, 2 percent by state and local governments, and 3 percent by patients. Under Health Card, 13 percent would be paid by the federal government and 2 percent by patients. Thus, taxes (federal, state, and local) would rise by 6 percent of GDP (from 7 percent to 13 percent), and the private share would fall by 6 percent (from 8 percent to 2 percent). Currently, the ratio of taxes to GDP is about 30 percent in the United States, 40 percent in Western Europe, and 50 percent in Scandinavia. National health insurance (which would replace Medicare and Medicaid) would raise the ratio of taxes to GDP to about 36 percent, several points below Western Europe."

"Am I right," asked the president, "that you want each household to pay a fraction of its medical bill, so it has an incentive to weigh benefit against cost? You want to avoid the Aroman problems, don't you? You don't like our current situation, where the average household has its entire hospital bill paid by its insurer, because then neither the patient, physician, or hospital has any reason to care about cost, and we have to impose cumbersome government regulation to try to cope with the symptoms of free hospital care."

"Exactly," answered the health economist.

"But what's to prevent a household from obtaining private insurance to cover the fraction that the government won't pay, so that hospital care stays free?" asked the president.

"Good question, Mr. President. Fortunately, the answer is simple. Under my proposal, the government won't pay anything if the person receives reimbursement from private insurance."

"What do you mean?" said the president.

"Simply this. When the provider sends the bill to the government, it must indicate that it is not submitting the bill to a private insurer, and must enclose the patient's signature making the same pledge."

"But then," asked the president, "why would a household want to buy private health insurance, when it now gets Health Card automatically?"

"The answer, Mr. President, is that it almost certainly wouldn't."

"But," worried the president, "the private insurance companies would no longer be selling much health insurance. I'm going to have a political problem with this. Won't these companies receive a serious jolt?"

"Not as much as you fear, Mr. President. There was the same fear in the 1960s, when Medicare for the elderly was enacted. But the government contracted with private insurance companies to handle bill processing under Medicare. So the insurance companies retained their employees to continue bill processing. The companies were no longer paid for being insurers, but they continued to be paid for being the bill processors. They adjusted to the change very nicely."

"So," asked the president, "would the government contract with these companies to handle the bill processing?"

"Exactly, Mr. President. Why should the government try to process bills in-house when an experienced apparatus exists in the private insurance companies? The government will provide the companies with each household's maximum burden and cost sharing rate, based on the most recent tax return. But the bill processing will actually be performed by the private companies. Not only that, the companies will bid competitively for the government contracts, so the bill processing task will be *privatized* even though the government is the insurer."

"That sounds much better," said the president. "Still, it would be even nicer for me politically if the private companies could continue selling the insurance itself."

"Unfortunately, Mr. President, we can't accomplish our goals with private insurance. Private insurance does a reasonably good job of providing coverage for employees in large firms as long as they are healthy enough to remain employed with the firm. But it does a poor job of providing coverage for employees of small firms, the self-employed, the unemployed, and the retired. The reason is simple. With large firms, private insurers agree to enroll all employees (whether high-cost or low-cost) for the advantage of enrolling a huge number of households at a single stroke. But for any household unable to take shelter in a large firm, private insurers insist on assessing the likelihood that the household will be a high-cost subscriber. Insurers then resist covering high-cost people, or insist on charging them very high premiums. Private insurers are financially driven to charge each household a premium at least as great as the household's expected medical cost, or simply to reject such households.

"The financial imperative to avoid high-cost households is the fatal flaw of any private health insurance system. Any household unprotected by employment at a large workplace knows that its insurance may be canceled if a high-cost medical problem develops. Any employee of a large firm realizes that a health problem may force the employee out of the firm. Insurance may be lost when it is needed most. Paradoxically, a system of private insurance cannot provide insurance against losing insurance when one needs it most.

"Think what would happen if everyone's medical cost were known in advance. Private insurance would break down completely. If the cost of insuring household H is definitely $20,000, a private insurance company would charge at least $20,000, or simply reject the household. Fortunately, medical cost is not known in advance for many households. But it should come as no surprise that private insurance fails for the minority who are likely, or certain, to be high-cost, and unable to hide in a large workplace. It therefore fails to provide peace of mind. People realize that some day they may become high-cost, lose their job, and be forced to stand alone in front of insurance companies.

"There's another flaw with private health insurance. Private insurance cannot offer cost sharing that varies with *household* income or consumption. Why not? The private insurers cannot get data on *household* income from employers. True, the employer might provide each employee's wage, but he cannot provide data on the spouse's earnings, or the household's property income, unless the employee turns over his tax return. But what private insurer, competing for business, is going to request that employees turn over their tax returns?

"So any cost sharing must be uniform. And uniform cost sharing is inevitably too burdensome for unhealthy low-income households. Employers and unions know this, so on behalf of their employees, they obtain insurance with little or no cost sharing. The public, quite rightly, will never accept significant patient cost sharing unless it is income-related, with an ironclad maximum burden. And private insurance simply cannot offer this kind of cost sharing.

"But with virtually no patient cost sharing, as the Aromans learned, the result must be wasteful utilization and cumbersome government regulation of providers. The only way to limit waste and regulation is cost sharing. The only cost sharing that is equitable is income-related cost sharing. And the only one who can easily obtain household income data is the Internal Revenue Service.

"So, Mr. President, we cannot solve our problem as long as we rely on private insurance. Fortunately, as we saw when Medicare came in, the private insurers are needed to handle the bill processing. They will have a major role to play, and will be compensated accordingly. The tax increase must cover this bill processing cost, just as today's health insurance premiums cover the same cost."

"Now," said the president, "let me ask a more basic question. The Aroman lesson is persuasive for food. But will patient cost sharing really work for medical care? Will the heart attack victim look up from the stretcher and whisper, 'This hospital charges too much. Take me somewhere else'?"

"Mr. President, if the patient cost-sharing strategy depended on economizing during emergencies, it would obviously fail. But it doesn't depend on this at all."

"Then how is it supposed to work?" asked the president.

"We don't want to limit emergency care. But we don't want a tenth day in the hospital if it's not necessary. Who should make this decision? After all, some tenth days are very necessary. If it is free to the patient, then he and his doctor have no reason to weigh the cost—several hundred dollars—against the benefit. So government regulation must come in and apply pressure, as it does under Medicare's DRG (diagnostic related group) system.

"But suppose, Mr. President, that the patient must pay a fraction of the cost of the tenth day—a fraction that is scaled to his income. Then the government doesn't need to apply pressure. He and his doctor will weigh benefit against cost."

"But," asked the president, "doesn't the doctor really make the decision? Why should he care about the financial impact on his patient?"

"True, Mr. President, during an emergency the patient is preoccupied with his medical problem, and the doctor is often completely in charge. Even when the emergency passes, and the tenth day is weighed, the doctor may unilaterally make the decision. Today, the doctor usually knows that his patient will probably never see the hospital bill, much less pay any of it. But under our proposed insurance policy, the doctor will soon learn that his patient cares about the hospital bill. The recovering patient, with the emergency behind him, may well question the necessity of a tenth day and the doctor who prescribed it. Even now, doctors are often eager to show patients that they care about them, and try to save them money when this can be done without sacrificing quality. Under our policy, they will do the same with non-emergency hospital decisions."

"I have a final, fundamental question," said the president. "Why should people like paying a fraction of every medical bill? Won't they prefer free medical care?"

"Mr. President, remember what we learned from Aroma. Sure, it seems nice to get something for free. But each person should recognize that if it's free, government regulation of choice becomes inevitable. We see it already today. Under Medicare's DRG system, the government pressures hospitals to pressure doctors and patients to shorten hospital stays by fixing the government's payment according to the diagnosis, regardless of the actual cost incurred.

"So free care, Mr. President, is not really free. It inevitably brings on regulation, and the patient is no longer completely free to choose. The patient must wonder whether the doctor is deciding what is best medically, or bowing to the pressure of hospital administrators, who in turn are succumbing to the pressure of government regulators.

"Only patient cost sharing can reduce government pressure. With cost sharing, government can usually let patients and doctors make unpressured decisions, because they have an incentive to weigh cost as well as benefit."

"But can we make people understand that?" asked the president.

"Perhaps not immediately," answered the health economist. "But people will like having a ceiling on the burden they must bear. And they may not even recognize that their employer is sending a health insurance check to the government instead of a private insurance company. Their take-home pay will usually be hardly affected. So, Mr. President, many people will still support this proposal, even if they don't yet grasp its most important advantage: preserving each patient's freedom to choose medical care with less governmental interference."

The Press Conference

The president once again stood before the microphone. But this time he took the offensive. He announced his new health insurance proposal—Health Card—and let his health economist describe the details.

"Then everyone will have a maximum burden that relates to his income?" asked the same Swedish reporter, with some hesitation.

"Yes." The president smiled.

"And there will be no gaps? The coverage will be universal, regardless of the person's job, or even whether he or she has a job?"

"Yes," answered the president. There was a long pause. Finally, with warmth in his voice, the president said, "I would be glad to talk more about it. Shall I?"

But the European reporters hesitated. Their enthusiasm from the previous day had vanished. For so many years, they had proudly asked Americans how the affluent United States could let people be financially broken by medical problems. And now, suddenly, the question had become obsolete. At last, the United States appeared on the way to being second to none in health insurance protection.

The reporters looked at each other. Finally, one raised his hand, and spoke when the president called on him.

"Mr. President, perhaps you might tell us how your country has achieved such a high saving rate?"

11 TARGETED SCHOLARSHIPS AND PUBLIC SCHOOL FINANCE

The extraterrestrial visitor, XT, seemed delighted by the mechanism called competition.

"My discoveries on Earth have been simply fascinating," XT exclaimed to his American host in remarkably good English. "But perhaps more than anything else, this mechanism you use to improve productive performance is absolutely astonishing. After all, who would have thought it would work best?"

His host seemed puzzled. "I don't understand," he asked. "Isn't it obvious that competition is the best way to achieve better goods and services?"

"Not at all," replied XT. "You think it is obvious because you are so used to it. But it's not obvious at all. Where I come from, everyone would be simply amazed. They would say that the best way to do something is to create a single enterprise. Let the best minds come together in the enterprise and plot its course. Then let everyone cooperate and get the job done. And by all means, don't let other enterprises proliferate and wastefully duplicate effort. One cooperative effort, working in harmony for a single goal, is surely better than many enterprises working at cross purposes, engaged in petty rivalry with each other."

"But," said XT's American host, "in the United States we call such a single enterprise a *monopoly*. It's not a nice word in my country. A monopoly feels little pressure to perform well, because it has a captive audience. Consumers must buy its product. They have nowhere else to turn, no matter how poor a job the monopoly does. And the monopoly knows it. So the monopoly slacks off. It retains unproductive workers. It innovates slowly. And it responds sluggishly to consumer complaints."

"I know, I know," exclaimed XT. "What a contrast between your economic system and the communist system of the old Soviet Union. I'll never forget my visit to Moscow in the 1980s, before the fall of communism. What long lines there were at the Moscow department store! The poor Russians! How they grumbled. And how naive I was. I thought they must be willing to wait this long because the products were so wonderful. When I finally reached the front of the line, I couldn't believe it. What shoddy merchandise. But the poor devils simply had no choice."

"But XT," said his host, "you should have expected it. The Soviet economy consisted of monopolies. Oh sure, they were public monopolies, run by the state, supposedly dedicated to serving the people. But a monopoly is a monopoly. Whether it's public or private hardly matters. When consumers have no choice, when producers feel no pressure from competition, the result is the same: poor performance, shoddy goods and services."

"How astonishing," exclaimed XT, "but you are right. I have seen it with my own eyes. It's not even close. Competition dramatically outperforms monopoly. You should be quite proud of your little mechanism called competition."

"We are," replied his American host, beaming, "we are."

XT's Confusion

"But," continued XT, "there is something that confuses me. I hope you won't take offense at the questions I am about to ask."

"Not at all," replied his host with confidence. "Fire away."

"Well," said XT slowly, "you have been telling me how

important capital accumulation is for advancing the standard of living, and how capital consists of human capital and knowledge capital, as well as physical capital. Am I correct?"

"Absolutely," replied the host.

"Now," continued XT, "schools are an important producer of human capital—of education—are they not?"

"Of course."

"And isn't it important to get the best possible performance from these producers of education?"

"Naturally," replied the host.

"In fact," continued XT, "wouldn't you agree that it is more important to get excellent performance from producers of education than from producers of say, furniture?"

"I certainly would agree," replied his host.

"So," asked XT cautiously, "please don't take offense, but why do you use local monopolies to produce education?"

The host felt struck by a bolt from the blue. He simply hadn't seen it coming. For a moment he was speechless.

"After all," continued XT, "you are engaged in an intense international competition over the future standard of living. Human capital—education—is going to be a key determinant of how you do in that competition. I would have thought that here would be the most important place to use your astonishing mechanism of competition to get the best performance possible. And to my surprise, I find this is one of the few areas where you tolerate monopoly. I'm afraid I don't understand."

"But," said his host, "when it comes to education, we believe that each community should form a single enterprise, called a public school. We believe that the best minds in each community should come together in this enterprise and plot its course. Then everyone should cooperate and get the job done. And by all means, we shouldn't let other enterprises proliferate and wastefully duplicate effort. One cooperative effort, working in harmony for a single goal, is surely better than many enterprises working at cross purposes, engaged in petty rivalry with each other."

"Why," exclaimed XT, "that's the way everyone on my planet thinks. Are you sure you haven't visited there? That's what I thought until I came to Earth and discovered your marvelous invention, competition."

"But education is different," said his host.

"Yes," said XT, "it's more important. All the more reason to use your best weapon, competition. Please forgive me if I quote you. Didn't you tell me earlier that a monopoly feels little pressure to perform well because it has a captive audience? Consumers must buy its product. They have nowhere else to turn, no matter how poor a job it does. So the monopoly slacks off. It retains unproductive workers. It innovates slowly. And it responds sluggishly to consumer complaints. Did I dream it, or weren't these your very words?"

"Yes, yes, they were," muttered his host. "But our local monopolies are dedicated to serving the community."

"Yes," replied XT, "but didn't you also say that a monopoly is a monopoly? Whether it's public or private hardly matters. When consumers have no choice, when producers feel no pressure from competition, the result is the same: poor performance, shoddy goods and services."

"Maybe I did say that," admitted the host reluctantly. "But our local monopolies are different. Our teachers and principals are very dedicated. And the consumers—parents—form associations that monitor the school. They do apply pressure. And there is also pressure from parents through the election of school board members."

"I am sure that most of your teachers and principals are dedicated," replied XT. "I am sure your parent associations and school board elections do apply some pressure. But it is curious, you will admit, that where it counts most—education—you have decided to use monopoly instead of competition."

XT's Voucher Plan

"Would you indulge me?" XT asked his host. "I have been so taken with your little mechanism of competition that I just can't help trying to figure out how it might be used in education. Maybe you're right. Maybe public monopoly is better in education. But do you mind if I give it a try?"

"No, go right ahead," replied his host.

"Good," said XT. "Now, I may make some false starts. But whenever you object, I will try to correct my plan to handle your objection. May I begin?"

"By all means."

XT began. "Why not simply end taxation for schools and let parents use their own money to buy education for their children? I'm sure private schools would spring up. Each community would probably retain its public school, but now the school would have to raise its revenue by charging a price—tuition—just like the private schools. So private and public schools would compete on a level playing field, and parents would choose."

The host smiled. "I can't blame you for making this mistake, because on your planet, each household has roughly the same income. So each has the same ability to buy things. But perhaps you haven't noticed, in your fascination with our competition, that here on Earth households differ greatly in income, and hence, in ability to buy things. So under your proposal, the rich would buy higher-quality education than the middle class, and the poor might not be able to buy any education at all."

"I see," said XT thoughtfully. "And this would be very unfair, I agree, because a child's opportunity, through education, shouldn't depend on his parents' income."

"Exactly," confirmed the host. "So I'm afraid we don't need to go any further. Competition in education would simply be unfair."

"Please, please," pleaded XT, "indulge me. On my planet, we like to solve problems, and we don't give up so easily. Let me see what I can do about your important objection."

After a long pause, XT spoke. "How about this? Once again, end local school taxes, so the public schools must charge tuition, just like private schools. But let the state government raise taxes, and then use the revenue to reimburse each household a fixed amount per child. You might call the amount a *voucher*. The voucher would ensure that even the poor could afford a decent education."

"Your proposal is better," admitted the host, "but it's still not good enough. While it would guarantee the poor a minimum education, the quality of education would still vary greatly with income. The rich would add a lot to their voucher and receive high-quality education, the middle class would add a little, and the poor would add nothing at all. So there would still be great inequality."

XT thought for some time. Then he exclaimed, "I've got it. Why not make the voucher variable? The lower the family's income, the higher would be the voucher."

"Is that feasible?" asked the host.

"Yes," replied XT. "The voucher plan would utilize federal income tax returns to vary the voucher with the household's income."

Economas' Objection

"XT, I would like you to meet Economas," said the host. "Economas teaches about the virtues of economic competition."

"It is an honor to meet you," said XT. "I am quite taken by your mechanism called competition."

"Yes," replied Economas, "it works incredibly well for countless goods and services. Ordinarily, I advocate maximum economic competition. But what I have to say may surprise you. For elementary and secondary schools, I think we already have enough competition and choice for affluent families. The affluent can send their children to a private school, but they must pay the full tuition. Clearly, there is a strong bias in favor of the neighborhood public school because it's free. But I think a good case can be made that such a strong bias is desirable. For affluent families, I think our current situation is just about right."

"Please explain, Economas," said the surprised host.

"Even though public schools are free and private schools charge tuition, in affluent neighborhoods the school board, administrators, and teachers all know that if they do a poor job, a significant number of parents will switch their children to private schools. The fall in enrollments will reduce tax revenues sent to the public schools, and this will eventually reduce the salaries and employment of administrators and teachers. So private schools do exert competitive pressure on public schools in affluent neighborhoods. Moreover, affluent educated parents are active in monitoring school performance and working with school administrators and teachers. So affluent parents pressure their public schools in two ways: first, they have the ability to switch to a private school; and second, they directly interact with administrators and teachers."

"Wouldn't it be still better if there were a level playing field between public and private schools, with all schools charging tuition, and none directly receiving tax revenue?" asked XT.

"I disagree," replied Economas. "Let me explain. To my children, it matters a great deal which school their friends attend. Economists call this a *consumption externality*. If my eight-year old son's friend gets a birthday present my son wants, he may be jealous for a day, but he'll quickly get over it. But if his friend gets accepted at one school, and he gets rejected, it would take a long time for him to get over it."

"I've heard that even high school seniors need some time to get over such an experience concerning college admissions," admitted XT.

"Parents and children," continued Economas, "care very much about who else attends their school. But for just this reason, competing schools will be selective in their admissions. They will act like colleges. They will have admission tests, accepting some, rejecting others. Just as colleges get ranked, elementary schools will get ranked. One eight-year old will get into a high-ranked school while her best friend is rejected."

"But couldn't the government prohibit elementary schools from being selective in their admissions?" asked XT.

"It could try," said Economas. "But I'm not very confident it would work. This would be a major change for our private schools that have always sought information about applicants.

They might prefer to stay out of the voucher plan rather than submit to blind admissions."

"It won't be easy to enforce blind admissions," said the host. "Schools will resist simply being assigned students by lottery. If they are allowed to interview the applicant's family, it will be easy to obtain information about educational background and occupation. Without a lottery, it seems likely that school rankings will develop, and rejections will split friends."

"Even if blind admissions could be enforced," said Economas, "there is still a problem. Today, youngsters in the same neighborhood usually attend the same public school. Friends can be sure they can go to the same school, and when friendships change, it will be among youngsters in the same neighborhood. These friendships are an end in itself, often lead to friendship among parents, and build a sense of community. But now suppose that neighborhood friends are admitted randomly to different schools. It's not as bad if the choice is random rather than based on test scores or grades. But it still splits friendships."

"I see your point," admitted XT.

"Economists call this a *consumption externality* because if neighborhood children are split among a substantial number of private schools, many children will be adversely affected due to rejections, split friendships, and a weakening of neighborhood ties. The externality implies that there should be a strong financial bias in favor of the neighborhood public school. A family should be able to switch to a private school—indeed, this threat provides some competitive pressure on the public schools—but the family should have to bear a significant financial burden so that switching is the exception rather than the rule."

"Is there any other externality that warrants favoring public schools?" asked XT.

"I think there is," replied Economas. "When children of different incomes, races, religions, ethnicities, genders, and disabilities attend the same public school, most learn to interact and work together, and this experience carries over when they enter the workplace and residential community. Employers may be more willing to hire and promote according to skill and merit, rather than according to race, religion, ethnicity, gender, or disability. There may be greater tolerance in political as well as economic life. While some private schools achieve this mix, many do not. Public schools are supposed to plan sufficient capacity so they can accept all applicants, and to treat all students as first class citizens. This philosophy may stay with many students when they become adults, thereby strengthening our nation's commitment to tolerance."

Economas' Targeted Scholarship Plan

"Does this mean," asked the host, "that you are against a voucher plan that applies to all families and all schools?"

"That's correct," replied Economas. "I favor maintaining a strong bias in favor of neighborhood public schools by keeping them free, financed by taxes. Affluent families already have the option of choosing a private school because they can afford private school tuition, and this option already applies some competitive pressure to their public schools. So I think we already have it just about right for the affluent. But I agree that there is not enough choice for non-affluent families, and not enough competitive pressure being applied to their public schools."

"So what do you propose?" asked the host.

"I propose a targeted scholarship plan," replied Economas.

"How would it work?" asked the host.

"First," replied Economas, "public schools would remain free, financed by taxes; a family's scholarship would cover only a percentage of private school tuition and the family would be required to bear a significant financial burden if it chooses a private rather than a public school; the percentage should be higher for low-income families but should always be less than 100 percent. Second, the scholarship would be targeted on non-affluent families; the scholarship amount would phase down to zero as family income rises from low to middle income. The plan would use federal income tax returns to scale the scholarship to family income. Third, the scholarship could only be used at schools that do not discriminate on the basis of income, race, religion, ethnicity, gender, or disability. The scholarship might be used at an accredited school with a religious affiliation provided the school does not discriminate on the basis of religion in its enrollment, and provided the Supreme Court concludes that its use does not violate the constitutional separation of church and state."

"Your targeted scholarship plan differs significantly from XT's voucher plan," said the host. "True," replied Economas, "but like XT's plan, it would still apply some competitive pressure to public schools that enroll primarily non-affluent students, and give some choice to non-affluent parents who are very dissatisfied with their public school. After all, affluent public schools are already subject to some competitive pressure, and affluent parents already have some choice. As an economist, I want to favor neighborhood public schools over private schools because of the 'consumption externalities' I explained earlier. But as an economist, I also want some competitive pressure applied to all public schools. Today, poor families are trapped—most can't afford to switch to any private school, no matter how bad the situation is at their public school, and the public school knows it. A targeted scholarship would make switching a real possibility, and create real competitive pressure on these public schools for the first time."

"But," said the host, "I wonder whether the most concerned parents will switch their children, while children with unconcerned parents will stay in bad public schools. These children will lose the positive influence of the better students and will be even worse off."

"I admit this is possible," replied Economas. "But don't forget a key point: The new competitive pressure on public schools in poor neighborhoods should improve public school performance. For the first time, administrators and teachers at these schools would worry about losing their jobs as a result of a fall in enrollment. The threat of concerned parents switching should improve public school performance and thereby reduce the actual number who switch. So I think it is more likely that children of unconcerned parents will be better off."

"But in some places the public school will stay bad," replied the host, "the best students will switch, and children with unconcerned parents will be worse off. Maybe we need to keep the best students in the bad school for the sake of the other children."

"Would you leave your child in a bad school for the sake of children whose parents don't care?" asked Economas.

"No," replied the host.

"Then I don't think it's fair for you to ask concerned poor parents to sacrifice their own children when you wouldn't sacrifice yours." said Economas. "Non-affluent families deserve some choice and some competitive pressure on their public schools—something affluent families already have and take for granted."

Reducing Inequality in Public School Spending per Pupil

"Something else is crucial for improving the education of the non-affluent," said Economas. "We need to reduce inequality in public school spending per pupil."

"I don't understand," said XT.

"In your fascination with competition, XT, you have overlooked a simple point," said Economas. "Affluent children get much more spending per pupil than non-affluent children."

"But," said the host, "don't we try to reduce this inequality by state and federal aid formulas? I thought that states give more aid per pupil to poor school districts than to affluent school districts, and that most federal aid is targeted on poor school districts."

"That's true," replied Economas, "but great inequality still remains. On average, affluent districts spend about 50 percent more per pupil than poor districts."

"Fifty percent is an enormous difference," admitted the host. "But is expenditure per pupil really that important for educational quality? Isn't the education and income of the families of a school's children more important?"

"That may be," replied Economas. "But the affluent already have their children in a school where parents have high education and income, so if expenditure per pupil doesn't matter, why do they choose to spend 50 percent more than poor districts?"

"Good question," admitted the host.

"The affluent recognize," continued Economas, "that higher expenditure per pupil buys higher-quality teachers, newer textbooks, better-equipped science labs, newer and better computers, and fewer students per teacher. It would be very odd if greater expenditure didn't yield higher educational quality. After all, it does for appliances, furniture, houses, cars, roads and bridges, hospitals, police, the military, and countless other goods and services. Why shouldn't it yield higher quality for education?"

"But I know some affluent people," said the host, "who insist that expenditure per pupil doesn't matter."

"Watch what they do," said Economas, "not what they say. They are free to spend the same as poor districts. But they don't. On average, they choose to spend 50 percent more per pupil."

"Maybe what they mean," said the host, "is that higher expenditure per pupil won't do much good as long as a school fails to maintain discipline in the classroom."

"That's where my targeted scholarship plan should help," replied Economas. "If families can afford to switch to private schools, there will be competitive pressure on public schools to maintain discipline. With better discipline in the classroom, greater expenditure per pupil will surely improve educational quality."

"But it's more than that," said the host. "Greater spending per pupil may not help much as long as drugs and crime are rampant in the neighborhood."

"I agree," said Economas. "Reducing drugs and crime should be a top priority. Once again, that requires higher expenditure on police, courts, and prisons, and much of this money must come from taxes raised outside the poor neighborhoods. The aim should be to help law-abiding, working parents in those neighborhoods who are concerned about their children's education and safety."

"But which level of government should try to reduce inequality in public school spending?" asked the host.

"Both the state and federal government," replied Economas. "Both already provide public school aid that favors low-income districts. But significant inequality remains, because federal taxes finance less than 10 percent of elementary and secondary education, while local taxes finance nearly 50 percent. The strategy should be to raise state and especially federal tax shares while reducing local tax shares for public schools. Perhaps earmarking certain state and federal taxes for public school aid would be helpful in obtaining political support."

A Computer Tax Credit for Non-affluent Families

"I have a different point," said the host. "The inequality problem is growing more severe because of the personal computer and the Internet. Affluent parents spend much more to make sure their children have a high-quality personal computer and access to the Internet in their own home."

"You're right," said Economas. "Suppose a student is assigned to write a history report. In the affluent neighborhood, the student sits down after dinner at her computer with her own encyclopedia and perhaps her own history book. With her computer, she searches the Internet to find additional information. Then she types her first draft on the computer. Later, she works on the draft to revise it and uses the computer's spell check. But in the poor neighborhood, the student has no encyclopedia, no history book, and no computer. Her only chance is the school or public library. If she can get access to an encyclopedia, a history book, and a computer with access to the Internet, she is in luck. Otherwise, she's in trouble. Even if she can use the library's encyclopedia, without access to a computer she must write her first draft by hand. Then she must write the final draft from scratch. She must use a dictionary rather than a computer spell check. Finally, she probably must do her work before dinner, because the school or public library is probably closed in the evening, and even if it were open, it might not be safe to come home in the dark."

"What can we do about this?" asked the host.

"We can enact a computer tax credit for non-affluent families on the federal income tax," replied Economas. "To claim the credit, the family would include the receipt documenting its purchase with its tax return. The credit would reimburse the family for a percentage of the computer price up to a maximum. The credit would phase down to zero as family income rises from low to middle income. The credit would be 'refundable,' so that if a poor family's computer credit exceeds the tax it owes, it would get a 'refund' from the IRS. For example, if its computer credit is $900 and its tax is zero, the Internal Revenue Service would send it a check for $900, just as it sends refund checks to many households. Remember, the computer tax credit never completely removes the financial burden on the family—the percentage reimbursed is always less than 100 percent. So most non-affluent families will try to take good care of their computers. Of course, here's one more reason to reduce crime in poor neighborhoods."

A Compromise

"One final point," said the host. "Some citizens favor voucher plans but oppose reducing the inequality in public school spending, while other citizens favor just the reverse. But you favor both a targeted scholarship plan and reducing inequality in public school spending."

"That's right," said Economas. "We need both. We need a targeted scholarship plan for non-affluent families to give some choice to these families and to provide some competitive pressure on their public schools. Affluent families already have some choice and competitive pressure, and take it for granted. At the same time, we need to reduce inequality in public school spending by shifting more of the financing away from local governments to the state and federal governments that can and do redistribute funds from affluent to non-affluent districts."

"You're advocating a political compromise between the two sides," said the host.

"Exactly," said Economas. "I'm appealing to public school advocates to accept a targeted scholarship plan in return for more generous state and federal funding of public schools. And I'm appealing to voucher advocates to accept more state and federal funding of public schools and a targeted scholarship plan. To reassure both sides, they should be enacted as part of the same package. One hopes both sides will support the computer tax credit for non-affluent families."

"What do you think, XT?" asked the host.

"I've learned," XT replied, "not to get too excited about any mechanism, however fascinating, especially when one doesn't know certain complexities of the inhabitants of a strange planet. Economas has persuaded me that unrestricted competition is unwise for elementary and secondary schools. However, I am pleased that Economas agrees that some competitive pressure does have a role to play in improving public school performance, and that a targeted scholarship plan would be worth enacting. I now see that reducing inequality of public school spending per pupil deserves high priority and that a computer tax credit would be warranted for non-affluent families. Incidentally, I've become fascinated with your computers and your Internet. We don't have them on my planet. Any chance of an inter-planetary connection?"

12 THE EARNED INCOME CREDIT AND LAST-RESORT JOBS

We've got two economic problems at the bottom of our economy. The first problem is this: There are adults who work full time, but their low education and/or skill results in a low annual income. This has always been a problem, and it has intensified during the past two decades because wage inequality has been increasing in both the United States and most other economically advanced countries. Most economists cite two reasons for rising wage inequality: technological change, and greater international trade with low-wage countries. It is not immediately obvious that technological change must widen wage inequality between highly educated and less educated persons. After all, new machinery generally raises the productivity and wage of all workers, and over the past two centuries many new machines especially raised the productivity of workers with little education. It appears, however, that recent technological change, often involving computers, has favored highly educated workers more than less educated workers. Moreover, advances in telecommunications and transportation have increased international trade with low-wage countries, and this tends to put downward pressure on the wages of less educated workers in economically advanced countries.

Here's the second problem: too many less educated persons, both adults and teenagers, rely on welfare rather than work. Some don't want to work for low wages, while others want to work but often can't find an employer willing to hire them. There's a lot of disagreement about where the fault lies, but there's widespread agreement that work is better than welfare.

This chapter proposes further expansion of the earned income credit to treat the first problem, and the provision of last-resort low-wage jobs to treat the second.

The Earned Income Credit

People who work full time for low annual incomes are assisted by the earned income tax credit (EIC). If you've never heard of the EIC, you're not alone. The minimum wage and welfare are much more famous. But the EIC is much better than the minimum wage or welfare for persons able to work. Let me explain why.

The EIC was enacted by Congress in the mid-1970s. It is a tax credit on the federal income tax. In contrast to welfare, it's available only to people who actually work. No labor earnings, no EIC. Imagine yours is a low-earning household with two children in 1996. Your EIC supplement is based on your household's total labor earnings. For each $100 you earn, the government adds $40, until at $8,890 of earnings the government supplement reaches a total of $3,556 (40 percent of $8,890). It remains at $3,556 until your income reaches $11,610. Then, to avoid paying supplements to everyone in the economy, the phase-out begins. For each additional $100 you earn, the supplement is cut $21.06. When your total income reaches $28,495, the supplement has been cut to zero. So if your household earns less than $28,495 of total income, you're entitled to some supplement from the government. The maximum EIC credit and dollar thresholds are automatically adjusted for inflation. If you do not have a dependent child, you can qualify for a smaller EIC supplement provided you are at least 24 years of age.

But what if your earnings are so low that you don't owe any federal income tax? You still can get the full EIC supplement. EIC is a *refundable* tax credit. This means that if your EIC credit is greater than the tax you owe, the government will write you a check for the difference.

There are two practical problems with the earned income tax credit. First, many low-income workers have never heard of it and don't realize they are eligible. The IRS has solved this problem for any household that files a tax return. It checks each return to see if the household is entitled to an EIC credit, and grants the credit even if the household has neglected to claim it. Second, some low-income households don't file a tax return. To reach them, employers should be required to notify low-wage employees that they can get an EIC check from the IRS, but only if they file a tax return. Employers should be glad to cooperate. After all, the EIC makes the employer's wage more attractive to the employee.

Why is the EIC better than the minimum wage? Because the minimum wage reduces employment. An employer may find it profitable to hire a less educated person if he can pay him $4 an hour, but not if he must pay him $6. You can pontificate all day about what employers should do. But the hard fact is that employers will offer more jobs without a minimum wage law than with one.

The EIC response is this: Let employers offer more jobs at low wages. Then provide a supplement for workers. This way we get the best of both worlds—more jobs, and higher incomes (wages plus the EIC supplement) for workers.

The EIC is also better than the minimum wage because it is targeted. Raise the minimum wage and you raise the wage of teenagers from affluent households, while you reduce jobs for low-skilled heads of households. Raise the EIC, and you raise the money that goes only to households with low annual earnings.

The EIC is better than welfare because it sends the right message. No work, no assistance. If you are capable of work, the message should be: Forget welfare, but you can earn an EIC supplement by working.

There has been some recent concern about fraud. For example, sometimes two separated parents claimed the same child. This problem has been reduced by requiring the child's social security number on the tax return. Other measures are needed to limit fraud. But the problem should be kept in perspective. After all, there is a fraud problem with much of the tax code and among all income classes. Methods should be devised to limit all tax fraud, including the EIC fraud. But concern about fraud should not prevent the continued expansion of the EIC, which improves the well-being of so many households with full-time workers but low incomes (nearly 18 million households received the EIC in 1996).

The EIC has been expanded several times since its inception in the mid-1970s. It began supplementing only $10 for each $100 earned; in the mid-1980s, the supplement was raised to $14; two major expansions in the 1990s raised the supplement to $40 for a household with two children. The expansions were supported by both liberals and conservatives.

The EIC warrants further expansion. The maximum supplement in 1996 is still only $3,556 for a household earning between $8,890 and $11,610. The government's official poverty threshold for a family of four was approximately $16,000 in 1996. So if a household head worked 40 hours a week for 50 weeks at $5 an hour (roughly the minimum wage), the household would earn $10,000, receive an EIC supplement of $3,556, and still be roughly $2,500 below the poverty threshold. We want less educated people to work full time even at minimum wage jobs rather than turn to welfare, drug dealing, or crime. We ought to be willing to make the EIC generous enough so that such a full-time minimum wage worker can lift a family above the government's official poverty line.

Last-resort Low-wage Jobs

To get people on the right track, we need to send a clear message: "Do the right things, and you'll be rewarded. Do the wrong things, and you won't."

Welfare sends the wrong message. Of course, welfare is necessary for people genuinely unable to work. But it should be only for them. If you're capable of working, the message should be: Forget welfare, find work. But what about people who genuinely want to work but say they can't find a job? Good question.

The best answer is that the government must make sure there are last-resort low-wage jobs available for anyone willing to work. Every locality should have a federally sponsored jobs center. The pay should be slightly below minimum wage. While there will be no means test, and anyone in our society will be eligible, most won't show up at the jobs center. No one will be envious of these jobs, and no one will want to stay in them any longer than they have to. But they'll provide some help until the person can find a regular private or public sector job. Without these last-resort jobs, society will be unable to stick to its message of "no work, no assistance." After all, there are some people who genuinely want to work but can't immediately find a regular job. We can't simply turn them away, especially if they have children. But if we cave in and make them eligible for welfare, then abuse will follow, and we won't be able to tell who really is willing to work.

The only good test of willingness to work is actual work. Last-resort low-wage jobs are the key to preventing abuse. People willing to work will take them, and people unwilling to work won't. Of course, providing such jobs will cost the taxpayer some money. But preserving the message—no work, no help—is worth it.

Besides, there's plenty of useful work to be done. Many streets and parks are filthy. A carefully screened applicant can be a helper in a day-care center in her own neighborhood. In fact, this would be a good option for a responsible mother of children who are under school age, because her own children can attend the neighborhood center while she earns her paycheck as an aide. If she does a good job, she may eventually obtain a regular job at the center.

A job opportunity should be guaranteed for both men and

women. If you're a teenage boy sitting on a stoop saying there are no jobs available, you can be told it isn't so, there's a place to go to earn a paycheck. If you sincerely want to work, you'll go. If not, you won't. Though the job has low pay, if you do the job well your supervisor will recommend you to a regular employer. Do it well, and you won't have to do it for very long. It will be the first rung of the ladder. Do it badly, and you will be fired, with a chance to try again next month.

The government does not necessarily have to operate the work projects. It may be better to have the government contract with private firms to run the projects. But the government must finance the projects. It must make good on its guarantee to provide anyone willing to work with a low-wage job. Only with that guarantee is it acceptable to end welfare for anyone able to work.

But consider a young unmarried mother who refuses to work, thereby subjecting her children to starvation. True, we can't let her children starve. But we can judge her guilty of child neglect. There must be due process. She must be asked, "If you can't find a job, there's a place to go to get one: the local jobs center. Will you do it?" As long as she goes and does the job she is given, her children will not starve. If she is not willing to take the job, then we have no choice but to judge her guilty of child neglect and unfit to have custody of the children.

Now, obviously, it is usually best for children to stay with their parents. And in most cases, the young unmarried mother will go to work to keep her children. But in some cases, until drug or alcohol abuse is overcome, it may be better for the children to have another home.

What about the unmarried father? He can get a last-resort job too. Suppose he refuses? Quite often the young mother knows who the young father is. If she can no longer get welfare but has to work to feed her children, she may try to get the father to take a job and help support his children. She may be willing to name him, so the government can pursue him for child support.

But suppose none of this works. Suppose teenage girls see that if they become pregnant without marriage, they face work, not welfare. Suppose they see that the young father often gets off, and the young mother must work to keep her children. It's likely that more teenage girls will try harder not to get pregnant.

Of course, low-wage jobs have trouble competing with drug dealing or stealing. So just as the government must provide last resort jobs, it must be tougher on drugs and crime. The carrot and stick must both be used. The aim must be to create an environment where a teenage boy says, "If I do the right things—go to school regularly, do my homework, stay away from drugs and crime, and don't father a child until I'm married and can support my child—then I will be rewarded; but if I do the wrong things, I'll be in trouble." Similarly, we must create an environment where a teenage girl says, "If I do the right things—go to school regularly, do my homework, stay away from drugs and crime, and don't get pregnant until I'm married and can support my child—then I will be rewarded; but if I do the wrong things, I'll be in trouble."

It sounds conservative to say: No welfare, and be tougher on crime and drugs. It sounds liberal to say: Government will provide last-resort low-wage jobs. But we need both conservative and liberal wisdom to make progress at the bottom of our economy.

INDEX

About the Author

Laurence Seidman is a professor of economics at the University of Delaware. He previously taught at the University of Pennsylvania and Swarthmore College. He has published technical economics articles in the *American Economic Review, Journal of Political Economy, Review of Economics and Statistics, Journal of Public Economics, National Tax Journal, Public Finance Review, Southern Economic Journal,* and the *Journal of Macroeconomics.* His most recent book is *The USA Tax: A Progressive Consumption Tax* (Cambridge: MIT Press, 1997). He has won the teaching award of the College of Business and Economics at the University of Delaware.